CAUCASUS

URUS

ZAGROS

MESOPOTAMIA

ARABIA

THE FOX
A Tale from Neolithic Shkārat Msaied

by Konrad Nuka Godtfredsen and Moritz Kinzel

Proceedings of the Danish Institute in Damascus 17

YAYINLARI

THE FOX - A Tale from Neolithic Shkārat Msaied
by Konrad Nuka Godtfredsen (Graphics) and Moritz Kinzel (Concept, Storyline, and Graphics)

Proceedings of the Danish Institute in Damascus 17

Content Development
Moritz Kinzel, Bo Dahl Hermansen, and Mette Bangsborg Thuesen

SCIENTIFIC ADVISORY BOARD
Marie Louise Jørkov, Pia Wistoft Nielsen, Christoph Purschwitz, Charlott Hofmann Jensen,
Lisa Yeomans, Amaia Arranz Otaegui, Tobias Richter, Leslie Quintero, Phil Wilke,
Lisbeth Valgreen, Ingolf Thuesen, Lee Clare, Cecilie Lelek Tvetmarken

Text by Moritz Kinzel
with Mette Bangsborg Thuesen and Bo Dahl Hermansen
edited by Cecilie Lelek Tvetmarken
Copyright is with the authors

Produced with support by

Uddannelses- og
Forskningsministeriets udlodningsmidler 2017
(Vedr. sagsnr. 7072-00003B)
Projekttitel: Grafisk formidling af forhistorien

and

the Danish Institute in Damascus
(project alias: 1125801001 and 1169521001)
Neolithic Shkārat Msaied - Graphic outreach

Printed by
12. Matbaa
Basın Yayın San. ve Tic. Ltd. Şti.
Kağıthane - Istanbul / Turkey
Certificate No: 46618

Production and Distribution
Zero Prod. Ltd.
Abdullah Sokak, No: 17
34433 Beyoğlu - İstanbul / Turkey
Tel: +90 (212) 244 7521 Fax: +90 (212) 244 3209

info@zerobooksonline.com
www.zerobooksonline.com/en

Copenhagen, May 2020

Dear Readers,

Graphic novels in archaeology are not a new phenomenon. Illustrations have always played a major role in visualising and documenting archaeological finds. However, the book that you are holding in your hands is slightly different. It does not only tell a story based on archaeological findings, and it is also not the typical adventure story of some researchers going into the desert to uncover treasures of unbelievable value. No, this book tries to look behind the processes that influence how archaeologists build their narratives based on archaeological remains. How does an interpretation direct the overall story and how do new finds and results of a study change the content of the story? Is there only ONE story to tell or are more storylines possible?

We are fully aware that this may be confusing, especially when interweaving a Neolithic and an archaeological narrative as we have done in this graphic novel. Here are some guidelines for the reading of this graphic novel:

a) Text written with a typewriter is related to the archaeological research;

b) *Text using Italics relates to the Neolithic narrative.*

The story we want to tell is built around the find of the skeleton of a 35-year-old woman who died some 9000 years ago and had been found during our archaeological excavations in building Unit F in 2002/2003 at Shkārat Msaied, some 16 km north of Petra, Jordan.

Enjoy reading and keep researching

THE ARCHAEOLOGICAL TEAM

of the Shkārat Msaied Neolithic Project

Since 1999, an international team from the University of Copenhagen, Department of Cross-Cultural and Regional Studies (ToRS), formerly the Carsten Niebuhr Institute, has been excavating and studying the material culture from the Neolithic site of Shkārat Msaied. The pictures show some of the members of the team, whom you will encounter in our story. Our work would not have been possible without our workmen from the Bedouin tribes of Al Amarin, Sayidin, Merasqe, and Mraye from the nearby village of Beidha as well as the Department of Antiquities of Jordan.

Ingolf Thuesen
project Director

Bo Dahl Hermansen
mortuary practices

Charlott Hofmann Jensen
chipped stones

Pernille Bangsgaard
zooarchaeologist

Mikkel Bille
perception of light

Merete Pryds Helle
finds and fiction

Moritz Kinzel
architecture

Marie-Louise Jørkov
human remains

Anne Mette Harpelund
ground stone tools

Mette Bangsborg Thuesen
beads

Mette Marie Hald
palaeobotanist

Aiysha Abu Laban
shells

Christoph Purschwitz
chipped stones

Pia Wistoft Nielsen
bone tools and faunal remains

Konrad Nuka Godtfredsen
graphics

Here you see some people from a Neolithic community living in the mountain area north of what is nowadays known as Petra/Wadi Musa in Jordan. They have a strong group identity as seen by the fact that most of them have the same kind of clothing, jewellery, and the same haircut. Only the 'wise' men and women cut their hair differently. This community herd a few goats and sheep, but still depend mostly on hunting and the gathering of wild cereals. In the mountain area they live in, only a few plants are domesticated at this point. In their 'neighbourhood' are a few other settlements like the village at a place (nowadays) called Beidha. However, although they might meet with these groups regularly, they maintain their very individual group identity. They practice transhumance – staying in the open forests on the cooler plateaus to the east over the summer and moving down to the plains of Wadi Araba or spending longer periods at their home place (nowadays called Shkārat Msaied) during the winter.

Life during the Neolithic is a challenge. New ideas, beliefs, and ways of life are taking shape. Attempts to cultivate plants and herd animals begin to be successful, creating a turning point after which hunting and gathering are no longer the primary source of food supply for many communities in the Near East. Sedentary life – staying in one location – starts to be the norm, but this does not mean that people are not mobile anymore. Procurement of raw materials, the movement of animals, etc., still lead people to move through the landscape. It is a life where daily activities and ritual practices most probably cannot be separated into different spheres and behaviours as we tend to do today. Things and beliefs are much more entangled. Life is cyclical or like a spiral – structured by repeating seasons, practices, and events.

The main character of this story is standing to the right of the group: A woman, about 35 years old at the time of her death, trained to communicate with helping spirits by the old wise man of her group. She died about 9000 years ago and was excavated in 2003 by Danish archaeologists at Shkārat Msaied. Her helping spirit appears to her in the shape of a fox, a connection that is somehow linked to her greenstone amulet, which she inherited from her predecessor.

This is her story, or a story told about her...

PROLOGUE

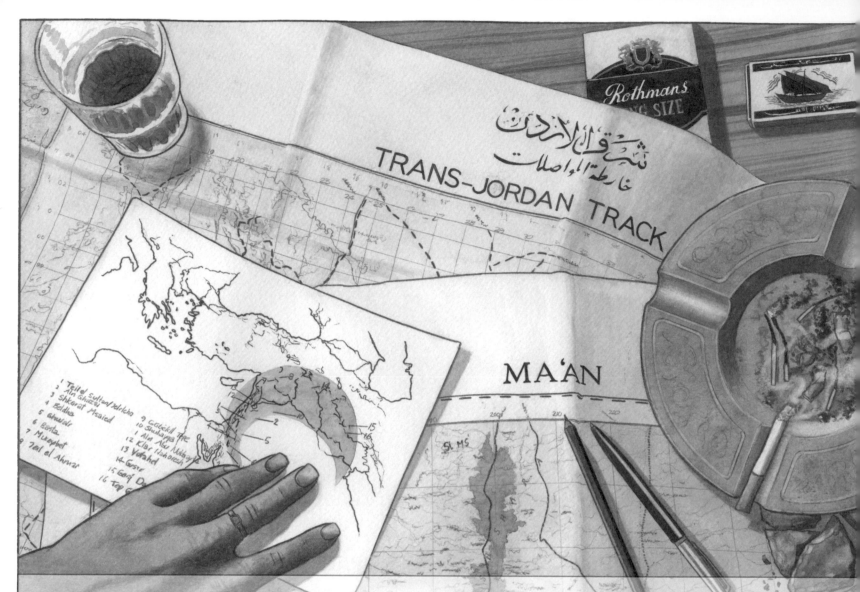

TRANS-JORDAN TRACK

MA'AN

"When the first researchers came to the Petra region in southern Jordan, we knew very little about the Neolithic in general and this region in particular. There is a set of behaviours and practices, including farming, herding and storing that is commonly referred to as Neolithic or could be described as a Neolithic 'lifestyle', which has developed in various regions of the Near East, including the Levant, Mesopotamia, and the Zagros Mountains. Some also call this area the Fertile Crescent. Back then the landscape looked quite different from what it does now. Because there was a higher humidity, the vegetation was much denser. We can subdivide the Neolithic into an earlier period without pottery and one with pottery. The first evidence of a Neolithic period without pottery comes from Jericho, or Tell es-Sultan as it is also known. Kathleen Kenyon called this period the Pre-Pottery Neolithic A and B. The Petra region in Jordan offers unique insights into the Neolithic world. The first archaeologist to survey and work here was Diana Kirkbride-Helbæk with her excavations at Beidha, just a few kilometres north of Petra/Wadi Musa."

1964

Shkârat Msaied

Excuse me, Ms. Kirkbride. More Gin 'n Lemon?

Well, Shkarat Msaied would be so interesting to study further, but I still have so much to do in Beidha!

...von hier geht es nur mit den Eseln weiter...*

1984

*...from here, we'll have to take the donkeys...

...schon vor 20 Jahren hat es Diana gespürt. Der Ort hier riecht regelrecht nach akeramischem Neolithikum B!*

*...Diana felt it 20 years ago already. This place really smells like Pre-Pottery Neolithic B!

De her sten lader til at danne mure, der må være omkring 9000 år gamle*

1999

*These stones look like they form walls, which date back 9000 years...

Og fundene tyder på, at der er foregået adskillige aktiviteter her. Lad os se, hvad udgravningen yderligere vil frembringe...*

*And the finds indicate that a lot of activities took place here. Let's see what more the excavation will reveal...

Det er 15 år siden, Hans Georg Gebel var her. Jeg kan godt forstå, at han er så optaget af dette område...*

*It's been 15 years since Hans Georg Gebel was here...I can understand why he is so interested in this area...

"The excavations at Shkārat Msaied began by setting out a 5 by 5 metre grid. The deposits were then excavated using various methods. All deposits, architecture, and finds were documented on Locus recording sheets and in diaries. The exposed architecture was drawn, and each context photographed. Soils were sieved, and sampled. Objects, bones, and scientific samples were bagged, tagged, and recorded on a list, which had to be handed over to the Department of Antiquities of Jordan and the Petra Museum at the end of each fieldwork season..."

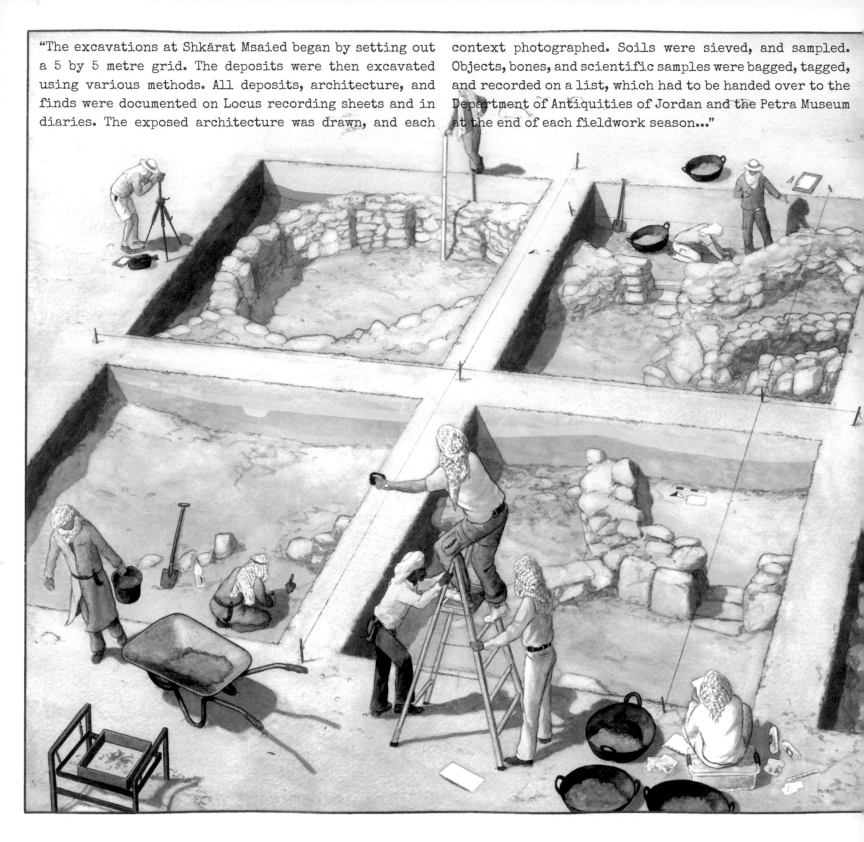

"So, what we imagine is our way of looking at how a Neolithic life could have been...and when you start to imagine it, then piece by piece a story starts to take shape..."

THE FOX

15

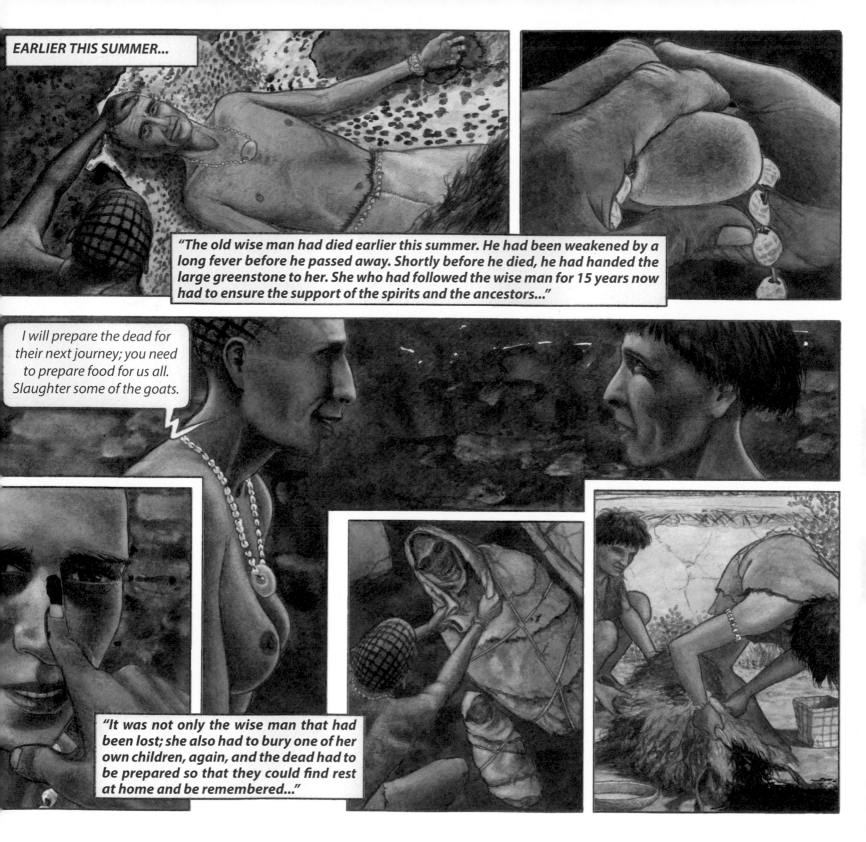

EARLIER THIS SUMMER...

"The old wise man had died earlier this summer. He had been weakened by a long fever before he passed away. Shortly before he died, he had handed the large greenstone to her. She who had followed the wise man for 15 years now had to ensure the support of the spirits and the ancestors..."

I will prepare the dead for their next journey; you need to prepare food for us all. Slaughter some of the goats.

"It was not only the wise man that had been lost; she also had to bury one of her own children, again, and the dead had to be prepared so that they could find rest at home and be remembered..."

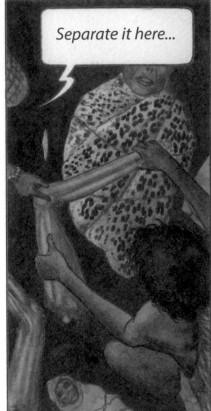

Did the feasting take place before the funeral or afterwards?

After we have lived and eaten together, now you must rest....
You have died – your house must die as well.
Let's light up the fire!

WINTER ABOUT FIVE YEARS LATER

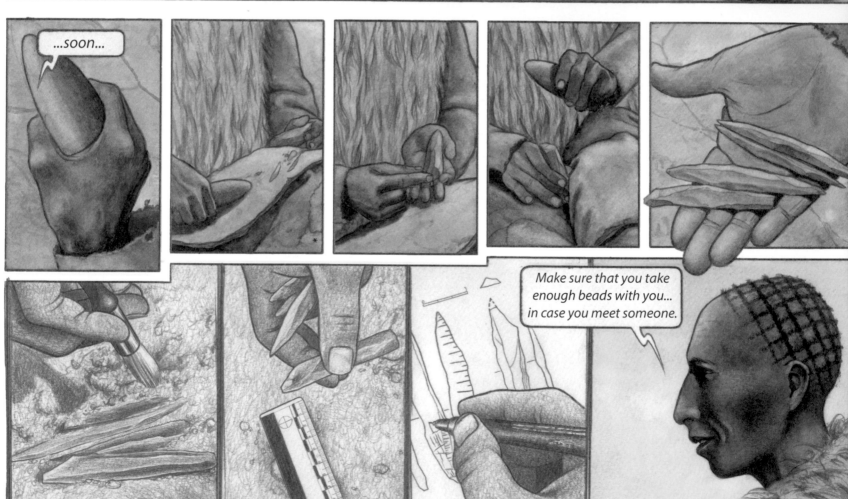

*Flint knapping sequence after Quintero (2010) and Purschwitz (2017).

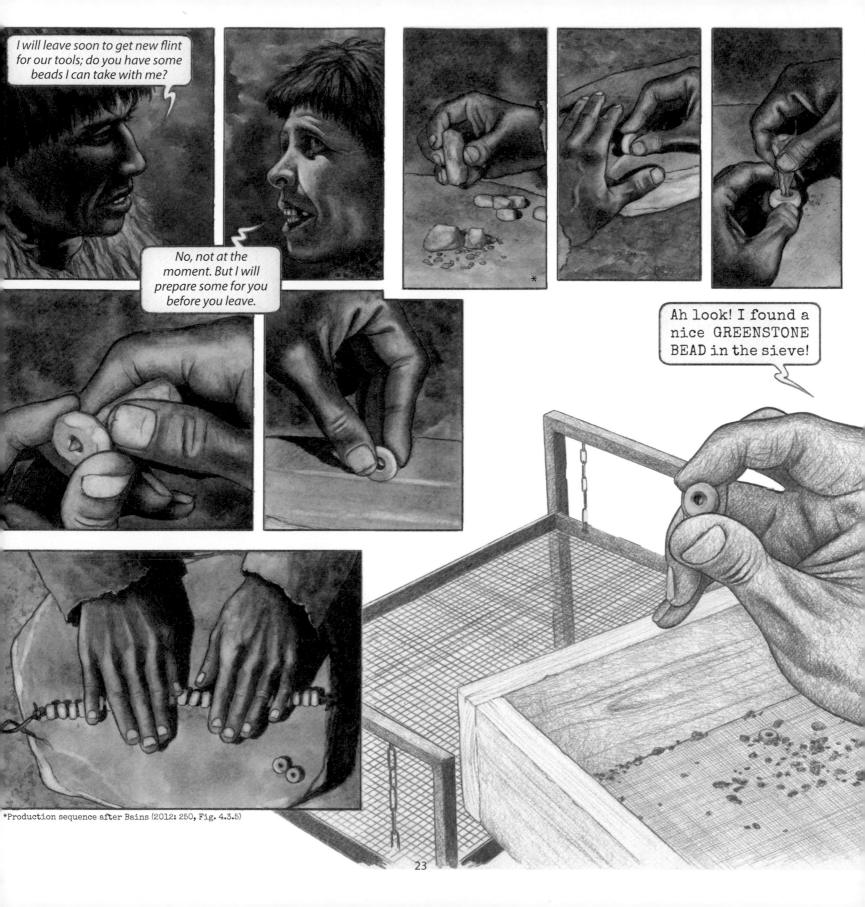

*Production sequence after Bains (2012: 250, Fig. 4.3.5)

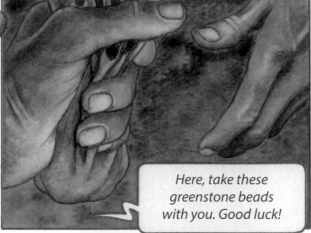

Here, take these greenstone beads with you. Good luck!

Return safely with the best raw material for our tools; we count on you!

Passing through this area always reminds me of our ancestors and their way of life...

You mean hunting mainly gazelle? Living in friable shelters? And...

24

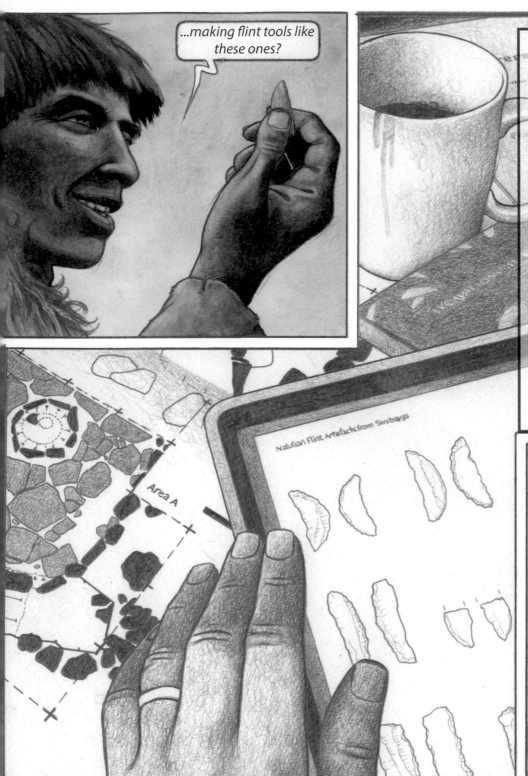

...making flint tools like these ones?

THE NATUFIAN

The Epipalaeolithic Natufian culture existed from around 13,500 to 9500 BCE in the Levant. This culture was characterised by a sedentary or semi-sedentary lifestyle, even before agriculture was introduced. The Natufian communities may be the ancestors of later Neolithic communities in the region. In general, the Natufian communities exploited wild cereals and hunted a wide variety of wild animals, including gazelles. The earliest evidence for bread-making has been found at Shubayqa 1, a 14,500-year-old Natufian site in Jordan's north-eastern desert.

Dorothy Garrod (1892-1968) coined the term Natufian based on finds from her excavations at Shuqba cave in Wadi an-Natuf, located in the western Judean Mountains.

Natufian Flint Artefacts from Shubayqa

Area A

Let us camp over there.

*For research on food remains see Arranz-Otaegui et al. (2018), and for more about hunting strategies see Yeomans et al. (2019).

26

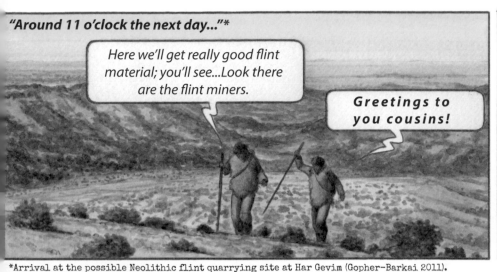

*Arrival at the possible Neolithic flint quarrying site at Har Gevim (Gopher–Barkai 2011).

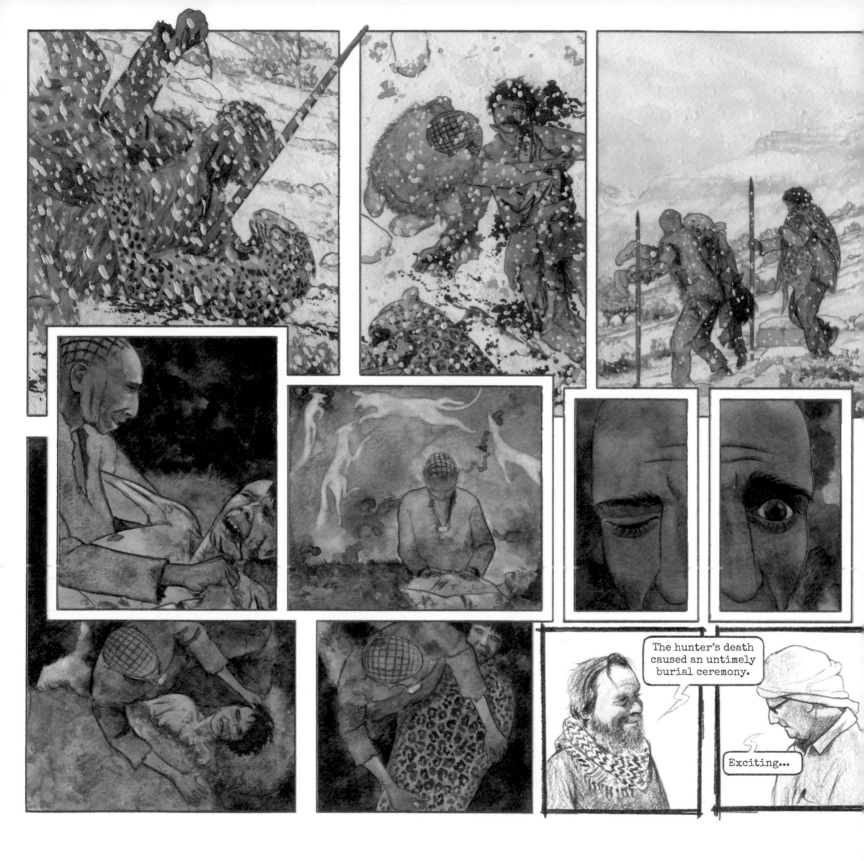

Preparing a burial ritual meant opening at least one of the burial cists, didn't it?

Oh no, all cists are full! The bones will need to be moved onwards... not sure if I like this to happen now. It will stir up the spirits...

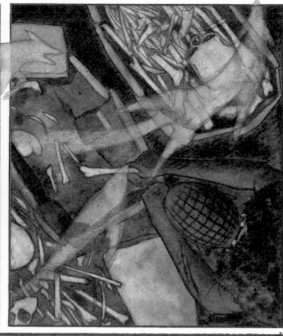

STAGE 2 – LIMINAL STAGE:

The dead are "in between and betwixt", hence a source of danger. Bones are sorted according to categories, dissolving individuality. Some skulls are kept separate. Placed in secure stone cists covered by stone slabs.

Stage 3 – INCORPORATION:

The dead have now been fully transformed. Human bones are completely mixed and even intermixed with animal bones. Bones of the dead could be removed or dispersed in floor fill.

The dead are now incorporated into a collective of ancestors. They may be considered as a source of life to society. A new cycle could then begin.

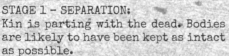
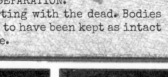

STAGE 1 – SEPARATION:

Kin is parting with the dead. Bodies are likely to have been kept as intact as possible.

35

37

39

LATE PRE-POTTERY NEOLITHIC B (LPPNB)
(ca. 7600–6900 BCE)

During the PPNB, the right angle was introduced into architecture. Complex buildings with multi-room arrangements as well as multi-storey buildings appeared. Dense, permanent settlements became common. The economy was based on farming and craft specialisation. The domestication of plants and animals was successful and the first experiments to produce pottery, in the region, took place.

41

*After Quintero et al. (1997).

43

* Colourful mineral pigments can be found in a deep and narrow gorge, nowadays known as Siq al Ba'ja.

"We found her a few days later..."

"... and cared for her in our home."

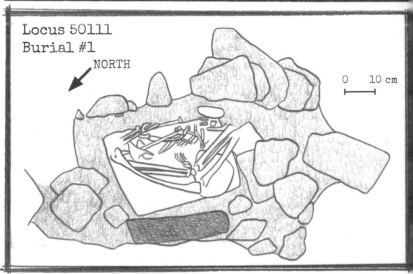

Locus 50111
Burial #1

NORTH

0   10 cm

46

"Then we blocked the doors...

...packed our things and left the place...

...to go to the summer camps up in the mountains and on the plateau...as usual intending to come back after the summer..."

...but they never returned.

EPILOGUE

52

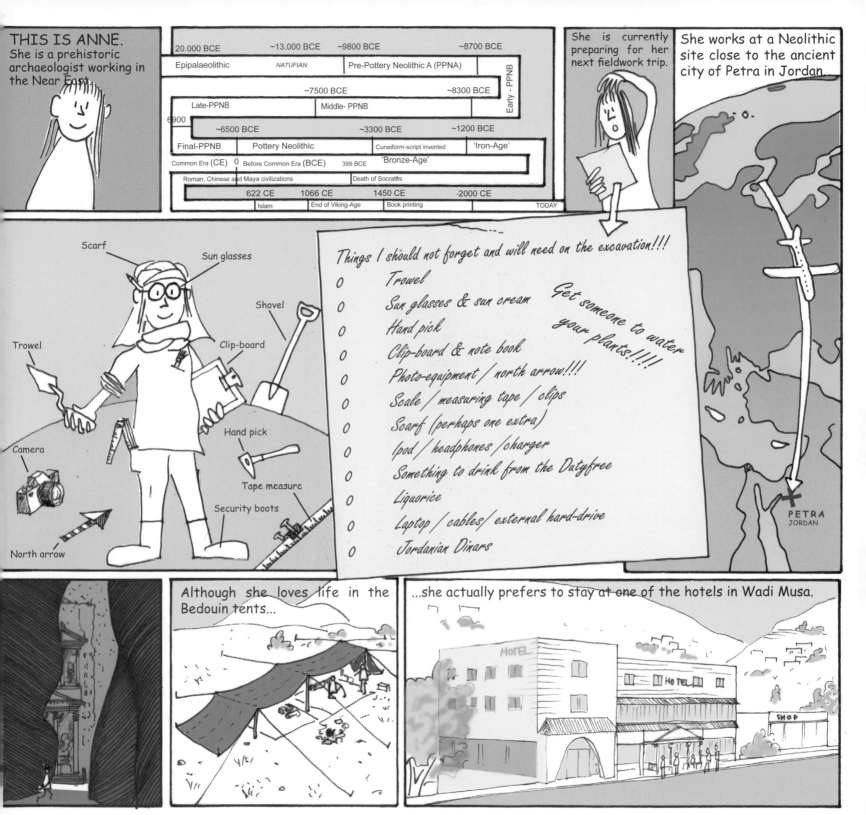

Every morning at 5:30 a.m. the team starts driving to the site.

It is still dark when they reach the site and meet with the workmen from Beidha.

This year Anne is working in an over 9000-year-old MPPNB roundhouse called Unit F.

Excavating is somehow different from the VR experience at home.

QR-Code Link to 3D-model

"Way too hot..."

...but her colleague the architect is still drawing his plans.

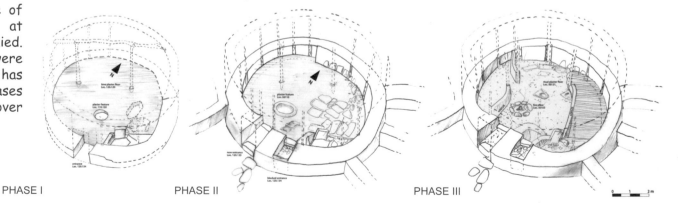

Building Unit F is one of the main structures at Neolithic Shkārat Msaied. Just about all burials were found here. Unit F has three main building phases and was transformed over time:

PHASE I

PHASE II

PHASE III

0   1   2 m

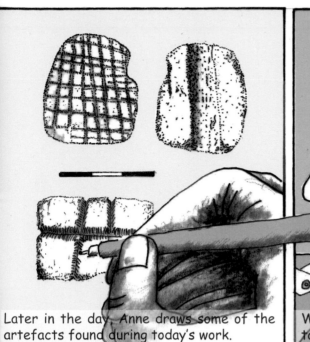

Later in the day, Anne draws some of the artefacts found during today's work.

While Anne is drawing, one of her colleagues takes photographs of the finds.

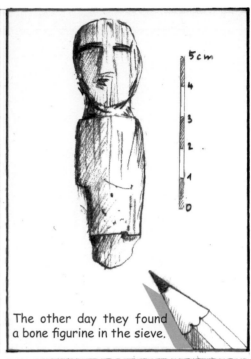

The other day they found a bone figurine in the sieve.

Can you imagine that a human produced this 9000 years ago?

...and when all the records have been entered into our database...

...we can analyse the finds statistically.

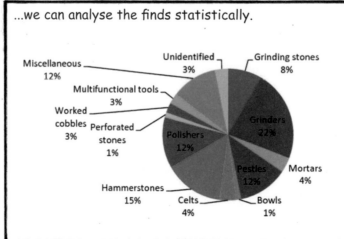

To do so, the archaeological record has to be very accurate and detailed...

First all the sediments are dry sieved...

...and afterwards most of the soil goes to floatation to catch plant remains...

...such as carbonised seeds and wood charcoal.

With a microscope, you can analyse the cell structure of the plants and identify the species: here – pistachio.

With this data we can reconstruct how the environment was during the Neolithic.

stone oak

pistachio

fig tree

juniper

2

3

1

4

Mia is studying the animal bones. They also tell us a lot about the environmental conditions as well as human-animal relationships. Mia sometimes wonders:

SM 2.15

Why are there so many bird bones? And what do the remains of fox and leopard tell us? There are images of these animals at Göbekli Tepe, a contemporary site in today's Turkey. These animals obviously played a role in the Neolithic mythology. However, the fox – a night animal and wanderer between the worlds – disappears from almost all mythologies in the region after the Neolithic.

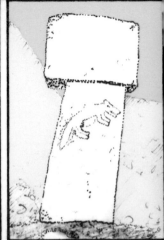

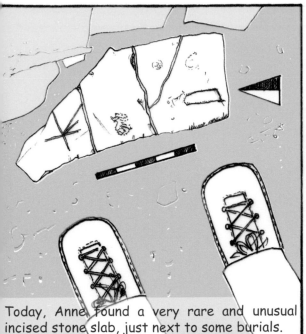

Today, Anne found a very rare and unusual incised stone slab, just next to some burials.

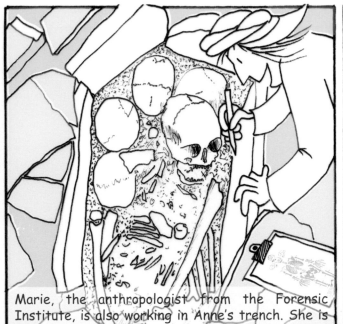

Marie, the anthropologist from the Forensic Institute, is also working in Anne's trench. She is excavating the human remains in the cists.

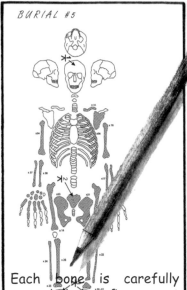

BURIAL #5

Each bone is carefully recorded to figure out how many individuals were actually buried in a grave.

...to be or not to be...

In the evening, the entire excavation team enjoys a Jordanian Mansaf.

Yes, this storyline would also have been a possible way of telling the story about the archaeological research at Neolithic Shkārat Msaied, but...

CONCLUDING REMARKS

NEOLITHIC STORYTELLING OR HOW TO TELL A STORY ABOUT THE NEOLITHIC

FACTS, IDEAS, AND CONCEPTS BEHIND THIS GRAPHIC NOVEL

by Moritz Kinzel, Bo Dahl Hermansen and Mette Bangsborg Thuesen

During our work at Shkārat Msaied, located close to the ancient city of Petra – nowadays Wadi Musa – in Jordan, we had many discussions about how life would have been in the Neolithic: what would a normal day be like, which birds would you hear in the vicinity, which smells would you inhale, and would it even be possible for us to survive more than three days?

When thinking about Neolithic lifeways, we also debated how we could present our various finds, interpretations, and ideas in an understandable way beyond the usual scientific reports. It was then suggested that perhaps a graphic novel could offer such an opportunity (see Macaulay 1979; Swogger 2015). Despite the fact that none of the archaeologists working on the project had made a graphic novel based on archaeological data before, we agreed that we would give this idea a try, not only to explore if such an approach could be a way to present at least some – if not all – aspects of the work conducted at the site, but also if this could be a part of the planned final publication of the archaeological work at Shkārat Msaied. Therefore, this graphic novel is in many aspects an experiment. The decision to produce a graphic novel also meant that we were forced to leave our comfort zone of well-formulated texts written in a hypothetical and academic manner. Instead, we had to make clear decisions on appearances, clothing, tools and their use, material culture, and behaviours – things we have little or no evidence for. The approaches presented here will always represent only one possible interpretation, though we nevertheless aimed to show a variety of options as the story unfolded.

In 2015, we had invited Konrad Nuka Godtfredsen, the artist of this graphic novel, to join us in the field to make some initial reconstruction sketches and to get familiar with the overall setting and colours of the area. In 2017, we received two grants for the project, one from the Danish Institute in Damascus and another from the Danish Ministry of Education and Research. We then started to collect and discuss ideas, possible scenarios, and a list of topics and locations we would like to include in a story that would take place at Neolithic Shkārat Msaied. However, the question remained: how to tell a story about the Neolithic? After some weeks of data assessment and discussion, a story evolved, centering on a 35-year-old woman we had found behind the standing stone in Unit F in 2002.

A first storyline was developed based on our initial ideas and the draft text was completed together with a collection of graphic material to illustrate the various topics and settings. Moritz Kinzel sketched the initial storyboard to test various possibilities and scenarios. The draft with sketches was then handed over to Konrad Nuka. The storyline draft needed adjusting when set out on paper and assembled into the actual graphics. Some scenes needed more space, others could be summarised or deleted. Sometimes it felt like editing a movie, which may demand an extra scene to be filmed or a long-planned sequence to be cut because it is hindering the flow of the narrative. Konrad Nuka got free hands to re-arrange the graphic sequence to ensure a good graphic flow and satisfying aesthetics. His draft sketch of the scene was then re-assessed by the scientific advisory board or specialist in question. Remarks and suggestions were noted directly on the drawings and send back for revision. This process was repeated – when needed – several times to get the best possible result. When everyone was happy with the result, the colouring process started.

During the work process, we realised that we could achieve the best result by looking at an entire episode at once and then going into detail. In this way, we kept an overview of the development of the full sequence. Thinking in entire sequences also helped speed up the process. Konrad Nuka worked with pencil and used watercolour to colour the drawings by hand. In some cases, Moritz carried out smaller adjustments with adobe photoshop in the post-drawing process. Moritz is also responsible for the epilogue presenting an alternative storyline and graphic style.

When working on the story we followed some basic guidelines to ensure a coherent content:

1) We examined our archaeological data and material from Shkārat Msaied to find primary information. If no information could be found there, we widened our research to include published material and finds from neighbouring sites in the greater Petra region, such as Beidha, Ba'ja, Basta, Wadi Faynan 16, Ghwair, etc.

2) If we could not find further information about specific aspects from those sites, we looked into the results from sites in a wider regional context (to the west, north, and east). We are aware of the problems of mixing different regional and local traditions into an 'artificial' Neolithic culture, which may not have existed, but our wish to rely on contemporary evidence served as a guiding principle here so as to provide the artist with enough background knowledge to create a convincing scenery.

3) Only in rare cases did we include additional material from outside

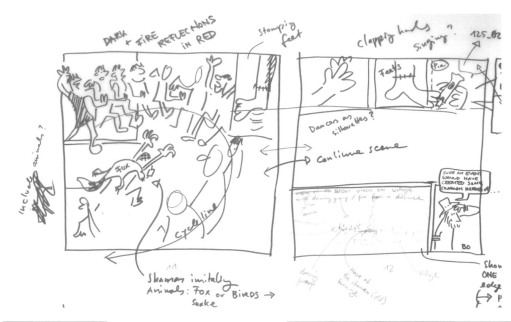

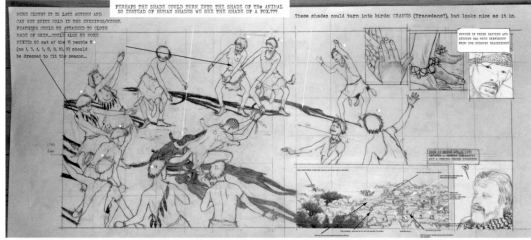

WORK PROCESS: Left: (top) Konrad Nuka and (bottom) Moritz sketching; Right: (top) sketched storyboard by Moritz; (middle) concept drawing by Konrad Nuka with comments by Moritz; (bottom) finalised page.

the Near Eastern hemisphere. This was done only to serve as an inspiration for, e.g. clothing or mortuary practices.

As previously mentioned, the story is built around a woman who died at an age of about 35 years. She was found on top of a stone feature (Loc. 50111) behind a vertically placed stone slab (Loc. 60116) in the round structure called Unit F at Shkārat Msaied. These human remains were discovered in 2002 and fully excavated in 2003 by Niels Lynnerup, a specialist in ancient human remains from the Department of Forensic Medicine at the University of Copenhagen. It was actually the first human skeleton to be excavated at Shkārat Msaied (Jensen et al. 2005). Her remains had been treated in a special way in the Neolithic: her skull had been removed and her long bones – still showing traces of ligaments and tissue – had been placed into her chest. Some goat mandibles had been buried alongside her remains, suggesting that some form of feasting had possibly taken place as part of a ceremony.

How does the woman and the fox go together? Fox remains were found in house Unit F and the contexts of the burials. None of them were complete, indicating that only specific parts were brought into the building. Foxes were part of the Neolithic 'mythology' as their presence on the T-shaped pillars at the Neolithic site of Göbekli Tepe (Turkey) suggests (Peters and Schmidt 2004). They can be seen as mediators between the 'underworld' and the world of the living. They are night creatures, wanderers, and in that way a (helping) spirit; clever and smart but also cunning and tricky. Interestingly, the fox disappears from the iconography (and also from the mythologies) of the Middle East after the Neolithic. In favour of what we considered a more engaging narrative, we decided to connect two components found in different contexts within the building: the remains of fox from a cache of skulls and a large greenstone bead found in one of the other burial cists in the same building. In the story the ability to communicate with the 'fox spirit' is bound to the greenstone bead.

Surrounding the woman's narrative are various interwoven life cycles: 1) the annual cycle of seasons (autumn, winter, spring, and summer); 2) the (human) cycle of life and death; and 3) the life cycles of buildings in the settlement; all of which are marked by a number of repetitive events and rituals representing the beginning or end of a cycle.

As the reader may notice, the story has various embedded narrative levels: 1) the archaeological researchers working on the site and trying to understand the finds; 2) *a Neolithic narrator telling the story about the woman – who turns out to be her former apprentice;* and 3) *some episodes of the life of the (headless) woman.* The narrative levels are intertwined and influence each other. In order to separate them graphically, the Neolithic thread is depicted in colour, while the archaeology is shown in black and white. *For the Neolithic, the text font is in italics,* while the archaeological part has a typewriter font. The epilogue and the alternative storyline are set with Comic Sans. It is important to keep in mind when reading the story that all these different narratives are products of our imagination and interpretation. They may be plausible but are still a construct of our time and context. A narrative is more accessible if the protagonist have names; but how do we name someone from the Neolithic? We have no information about their language, what their names for locations may have been, or their perception of space, and no information about whether people had names at all. In what kind of social communities and units did they live together? How were they related? So far, we have not been able to extract any genetic material as the preservation of DNA at Shkārat Msaied was not good enough to enable an analysis. Because of all these uncertainties and to avoid any later cultural connections, we decided not to use names. Instead, we decided to refer to the main protagonist as just 'the woman' although it should be noted that we have no idea if people defined themselves through their biological gender or shared our modern perception of gender during the Neolithic. For the same reasons, we tried to keep the story as 'gender neutral' as possible when it came to depicting clothing, hair styles, and the division of labour.

SHKĀRAT MSAIED - SITE SETTING AND LOCATION

The Neolithic site of Shkārat Msaied is located in the sandstone mountain area in the Nemelleh region, about 16 km north of Wadi Musa/Petra in southern Jordan. It belongs to the Middle Pre-Pottery Neolithic B (MPPNB) period, which dates between 8340 BCE and 7960 BCE. One older date (Sample number Aar 9336: 9150–8830 BCE) may hint at an earlier phase of occupation at the site. The site had probably also been visited during the Epipalaeolithic because of its location on a high pass from the east into the Rift valley (Hermansen et al. 2006). This well-preserved site is of archaeological and historical importance because it was inhabited in a period marked by crucial developments in subsistence strategies as people began to experiment with cultivation of plants and herding of animals. The (nowadays) semi-arid landscape in which the site is situated was mainly occupied by mobile hunter-gatherer groups in the Neolithic who lived in circular buildings that were more substantial than in previous periods and who had a rich and diverse material culture. The site is interpreted as a seasonal camp that was visited from autumn to spring, on the way to and from the open forests in the mountains. This is supported by the fact that most of the entrances were found blocked with stones (Kinzel 2013) and because the animal bone assemblage from Shkārat Msaied has a high number

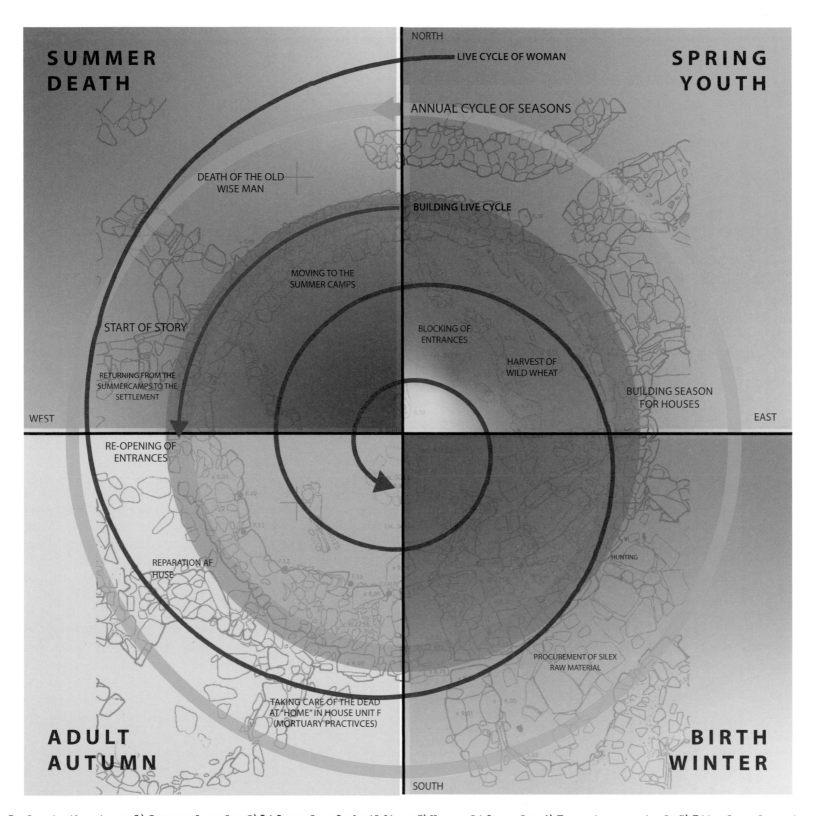

NORTH

SUMMER
DEATH

SPRING
YOUTH

LIVE CYCLE OF WOMAN

ANNUAL CYCLE OF SEASONS

DEATH OF THE OLD
WISE MAN

BUILDING LIVE CYCLE

MOVING TO THE
SUMMER CAMPS

START OF STORY

BLOCKING OF
ENTRANCES

HARVEST OF
WILD WHEAT

RETURNING FROM THE
SUMMERCAMPS TO THE
SETTLEMENT

BUILDING SEASON
FOR HOUSES

WEST

EAST

RE-OPENING OF
ENTRANCES

REPARATION AF
HUSE

HUNTING

PROCUREMENT OF SILEX
RAW MATERIAL

TAKING CARE OF THE DEAD
AT "HOME" IN HOUSE UNIT F
(MORTUARY PRACTIVCES)

ADULT
AUTUMN

BIRTH
WINTER

SOUTH

Cycles in the story: 1) Seasonal cycle; 2) Life cycle of a building; 3) Human life cycle; 4) Experience spiral; 5) Ritual cycles; etc .

63

of migrating raptors, e.g. black kites, which are only passing through the area in certain times of the year (Bangsgaard 2005).

ON RESEARCH HISTORY

The site was first surveyed by Diana Kirkbride-Helbæk in 1964 during her fieldwork at Neolithic Beidha, situated just 6 km south of Shkārat Msaied. The site was re-located and tested by Hans Georg Gebel in 1984 during his regional survey for the 'Tübinger Atlas des Vorderen Orients' (TAVO) (Gebel 2002). The site has been under excavation since 1999 by a Danish team from the Department of Cross-Cultural and Regional Studies (formerly the Carsten Niebuhr Institute) at the University of Copenhagen, first as a field school, with Lea Kaliszan (1999-2000) and Susanne Kerner (2001) as field directors, and then as a research project.

To set the scene for the Neolithic narrative and to introduce the archaeological site of Shkārat Msaied, we decided to open with a sequence highlighting some aspects of the research history of the site. Given the site's proximity to Petra, it was hard to resist an Indiana Jones inspired introduction. However, the flight scene is technically incorrect as Diana Kirkbride-Helbæk did not travel by plane to Jordan. First of all, there were only a few flights to this destination in those years and these would have been way too expensive for a young scholar like her. She actually went back and forth by a cheap bus and boat ride:

"You see there weren't these planes. We used to do what we called the Bus Run, the Sixpenny Sick from Beirut to Cyprus to Alexandria to Athens to Genoa to Marseilles – it was hardly a cruise in those ships – most of them at the bottom of the deep blue sea now – thoroughly unseaworthy, all under flags of convenience" (Kirkbride-Helbæk in an interview in 1994).

In 1963 she bought a new VW Beetle, which she drove from Lebanon to Turkey and back to Jordan. She discovered the Neolithic site of Shkārat Msaied while on a survey in April 1964. Her expedition had *"twelve camels and their masters, four donkeys, one white horse, a soldier from the Camel Corps, a Department of Antiquities man, Mo[hammed], and a Jericho man [...]"* and a dog (Diana Kirkbride-Helbæk in a letter dated 17.04.1964). Dr Hans Georg Gebel, on the other hand, came by donkeys to Shkārat Msaied in 1984. The artist, however, envisioned this differently and did not want to discard the Land Rover once it had been set onto paper. Gebel did a brief survey of the site and excavated a test pit (Gebel 1988). The Danish team arrived in 1999 with rental cars after a bulldozer was paid to create a dirt road that would enable a water tank truck to come to the site in

order to ensure the water supply for the field school. The team staye in Bedouin tents on site, going to Wadi Musa only on the weekend In 2002 the University's field school moved to Jerash and the wor at Shkārat Msaied continued as a research project with graduat students until the present (Jensen et al. 2005; Hermansen et al. 200(Kinzel et al. 2010; Kinzel 2019). Between 2003 and 2005, the wor was supported by a grant from the Carlsberg Foundation. Works i 2007, 2010, and 2014 to 2016 were supported by grants from th Danish Institute in Damascus, the Danish Palestine Foundatior and the Department of Cross-Cultural and Regional Studies (ToRS University of Copenhagen. During the field school, the team staye in tents on site and shared a house in Beidha. In the years after, w shared a dig house in Beidha with the German research society e *oriente e.V.* – working at Neolithic Ba'ja – and stayed at the Al Anba Hotel in Wadi Musa.

ON THE APPEARANCE OF PROTAGONISTS

To depict Neolithic people is difficult given that little is know about their appearance. It has not been possible to trace the ski colour, hair, and eye colour yet due to the often poor preservatio of the surviving bone material. Furthermore, the bone material i unfortunately not preserved well enough to enable the extractio of collagen necessary to analyse the genetic information. Th lack of DNA material has reduced what we know about the actua appearance of the inhabitants at Shkārat Msaied. The skin colour an appearance of hair and eye colour as presented in the graphic nove are speculative. We discussed whether to use black and white image for the Neolithic storyline and colours for the archaeologists in orde to avoid the colour debate but realised that we would actually onl have skirted the debate as shading for the skin would still have bee needed. The darker shade, which we finally decided on using, reflect the idea that Neolithic communities led a predominantly outdoo life, which would have led to prolonged exposure to sunlight.

The human bone material suggests that there was a large variety i shape and height within the population. In one of the burials (Locu 80316), we had one very large male (partially decomposed whe buried) who measured approximately 173–179 cm. Other lon bones of males indicate a slightly lower height at around 164–17(cm. Females were about 10 cm shorter than the males (152–15 cm). The people appeared to have been quite muscular, perhap even bulky. Some bones had marked muscle attachments, meanin that they were muscularly built, and although we were not able t establish the sex, they were most probably from males. Some ha degenerative changes in their neck or lower back. The changes i the neck may stem from carrying stuff on their head; but it could als

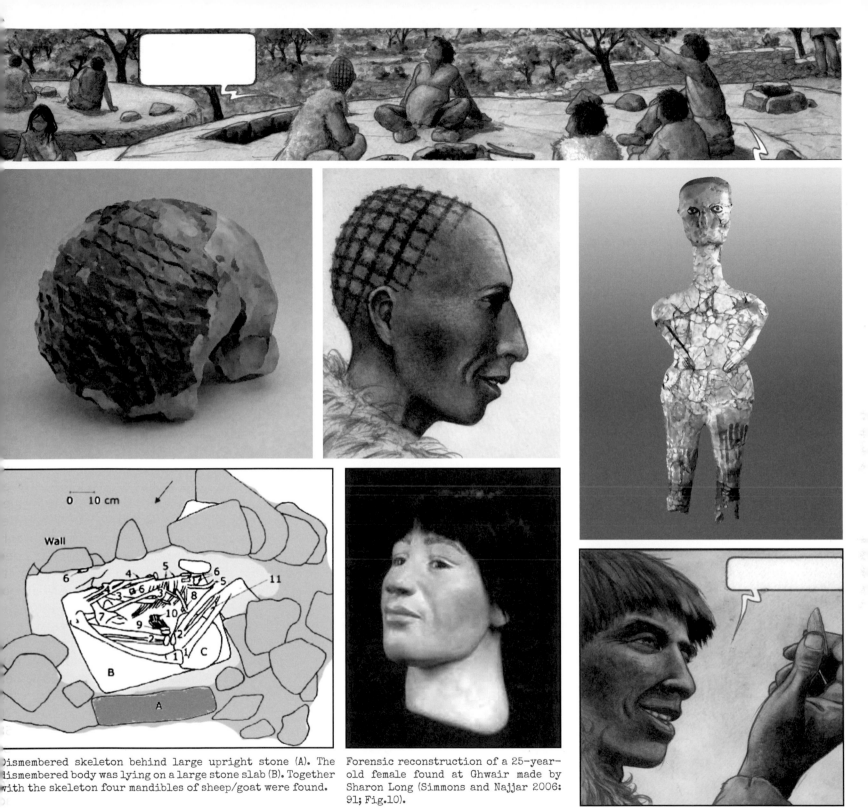

Dismembered skeleton behind large upright stone (A). The dismembered body was lying on a large stone slab (B). Together with the skeleton four mandibles of sheep/goat were found.

Forensic reconstruction of a 25-year-old female found at Ghwair made by Sharon Long (Simmons and Najjar 2006: 91; Fig.10).

The appearance of the Neolithic protagonists is inspired by the possible hairstyle on the skull from Nahal Hemar (after Bar-Yosef 1985) and the statues from Ain Ghazal and Jericho with their body painting and short hair (after National Museum of Jordan, Amman) as well as the analyses of the human remains excavated at Shkārat Msaied.

be just normal changes that come with age. Some smaller changes in the finger bones, possibly due to age, are visible as well. Many of the excavated individuals displayed quite heavy dental wear and it seems that they used their teeth as tools, although there was no clear evidence what these tasks may have been. The health condition of the Neolithic people at Shkārat Msaied was, according to Marie Louise Jørkov, our forensic anthropologist, 'not ideal' as the bones from some individuals show traces of malnutrition.

It is possible to draw some inspiration from the plastered skulls found at several Neolithic sites, e.g. Jericho (Kenyon 1953) and 'Ain Ghazal (Schmandt-Besserat 2013), which may provide hints regarding possible haircuts. Furthermore, the human statues found at 'Ain Ghazal show traces of what may be interpreted as body painting. A statue found at Jericho has some red lines suggesting a haircut, which we decided to use for the group staying at Shkārat Msaied. The Nahal Hemar skull (Bar-Yosef 1985) features a hairnet or afro style haircut (Fig. 5). This net-like hairstyle can be found as well on the so-called Nevali Çori-'totem pole' (Hauptmann 2011). This hairdo is somehow unique and seems to denote a 'special' person that could perhaps be associated with the role we had envisioned for our main character. Therefore, we decided to present this net-like hairstyle as a shaved haircut for our female main character. We debated if the other people should be left bald to avoid the haircut debate, but how would we then deal with other aspects where the evidence is limited? Would the people consequently run around naked only because we have no evidence for clothing? Clothing is one of the most difficult aspects when it comes to the graphics as they were made from perishable materials that do not survive in the archaeological record (Walter 2009; Grömer 2010).

Clothing was probably made from materials such as skin, leather, fur, wool, and maybe even linen. We decided on clothing that would reflect the seasons, the weather, and the activities being undertaken. In a way we had the challenge of finding a balance between nudity and textiles; between artistic imagination and scientific facts. Some might argue that it would be more suitable to show the Neolithic people with bodies showing traces of emaciation and starvation and women with sagging breasts. On the other hand, it is also difficult to say if we actually show too little nudity to meet the Neolithic reality (see Schrenk 2009; Siennicka et al. 2018; Levy 2020).

The case of the iceman 'Ötzi', although younger in date than Shkārat Msaied, shows nicely that Neolithic people had developed a very distinct use of skins and fibres (Fleckinger 2007; Sulzbacher 2008). The clothing is far from primitive and actually quite elaborated and well-adapted to the climatic conditions and to functionality.

However, for PPNB Shkārat Msaied most thoughts regarding clothing are currently highly speculative. The presence of bone tools such as awls and needles, suggests that at least skin and fur were being processed (Stordeur 1988). The presence of wings bones from birds suggests perhaps that feathers were used as decoration as well (Bangsgaard 2003).

ON ARCHITECTURE

The architecture at Shkārat Msaied follows the architectural tradition of earlier periods. Due to the mountain setting, some architectural developments obviously took place later here than at other settlements. On the other hand, you could also say that there may not have been an immediate need for change. As the studies by Moritz Kinzel (2013), who specialises in building archaeology, have shown, there are at least five building phases and complete modifications of the buildings having taken place. The architecture has been extensively studied, but there are always aspects of the building and maintenance processes that remain obscure.

In general, the buildings at Shkārat Msaied are single-roomed roundhouse structures with flat roofs. Similar houses have been excavated at the nearby contemporaneous site of Beidha (Byrd 2005). The roundhouse structure that is constructed in the story is a generic and idealised building that incorporates various elements of the architecture found at Shkārat Msaied (P.35-39). The double-faced stone walls were constructed around a wooden scaffold which carried the earthen roof. Wall stones were set into a mud mortar, which contained re-used plaster fragments, bone fragments and plant remains. The house structures were between three and seven metres in diameter and the interior spaces were on average about 2.20 metres high (Kinzel 2013; 2019). According to the finds from building Unit K, the roofs appear to have been flat earthen roofs. Much of daily life took place on the roofs and they served as one of the main activity areas within the settlement. Heavy ground stone tools, fireplaces, and flint tool workshops were found here. The interiors were relatively dark, and the only light source may have been the entrance and some small openings in the roofs. However, one concept of early architecture seems to be that (sun) light was excluded from the interior. It was a dim, closed space that kept out the bright light of the sun. We have found no evidence of lamps so far, although some flint 'bowl-lets' may be interpreted as such (Wilke et al. 2014). The interior of a typical house at Shkārat Msaied had a fine lime plaster floor. These floors are in general white-grey in colour, although a red-pigmented floor was found in Unit C. Set into the plaster floor in front of and aligned along the axis of the entrance was a depression with a raised rim of unknown function. On the

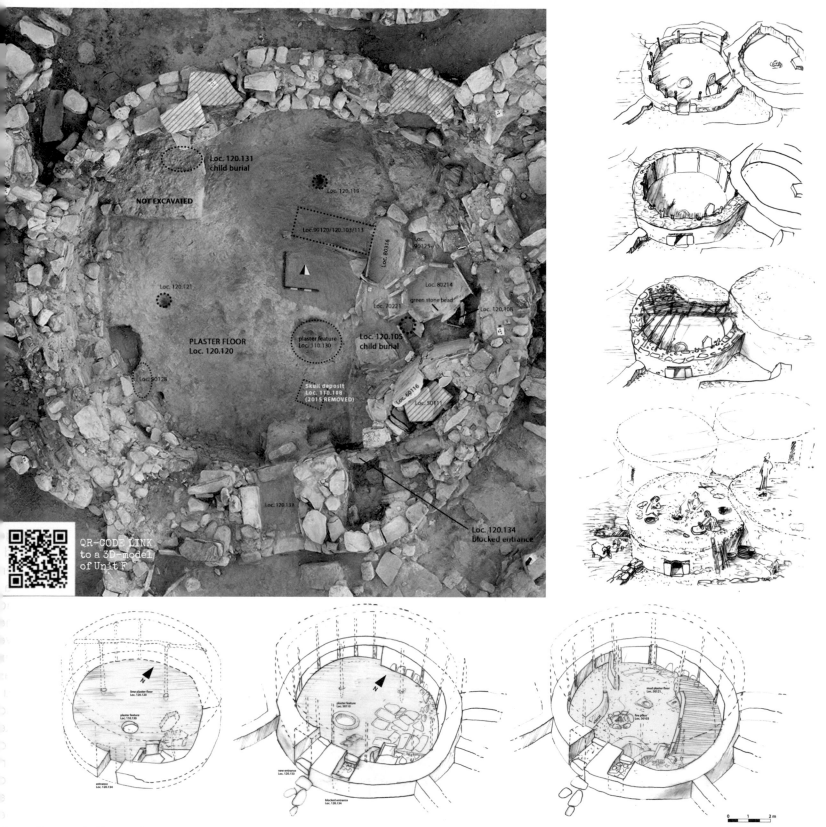

Loc. 120.131
child burial

NOT EXCAVATED

Loc. 120.119

Loc. 90120/120.103/113

Loc. 80316

Loc. 99125

Loc. 80214
green stone bead

Loc. 70221

Loc. 120.108

Loc. 120.105
child burial

Loc. 120.121

PLASTER FLOOR
Loc. 120.120

plaster feature
Loc. 110.130

Loc. 90128

Skull deposit
Loc. 110.108
(2015 REMOVED)

Loc. 60116

Loc. 50111

Loc. 120.133

Loc. 120.134
blocked entrance

QR-CODE LINK
to a 3D-model
of Unit F

lime plaster floor
Loc. 120.120

plaster feature
Loc. 110.130

entrance
Loc. 120.134

N

plaster feature
Loc. 90103

new entrance
Loc. 120.133

blocked entrance
Loc. 120.134

N

mud plaster floor
Loc. 50121

fire place
Loc. 50103

0   1   2 m

Roundhouse UNIT F is from the Middle PPNB and served as a mortuary house for a long period of time. The houses are built with rubble stone walls around a wooden scaffold carrying a flat roof, where the daily life took place (all graphics by M.Kinzel).

right-hand side when entering a building was a built-in feature: a stone box, a platform, a vertically placed, colourful sandstone slab, or a combination of these three features. Interior wall faces were plastered with mud or lime plaster. The evidence for exterior wall plaster is less clear.

Some of the interiors of the round structures had been modified over time into rectangular spaces. This transformation took place only internally. The full modification into rectangular buildings has not been recorded at Shkārat Msaied yet, but at nearby Beidha, which was excavated by Diana Kirkbride-Helbæk (Kirkbride 1966; Byrd 2005). The transformation from round to rectangular architecture is presented in the story by two children discussing and sketching different ground plans as have been documented at various Neolithic sites, e.g. Jerf el-Ahmar in Syria (Stordeur 2015) and Aşıklı in Central Anatolia/Turkey (Özbaşaran et al. 2018).

The endurance of the right angle in architecture after its introduction is represented in the story by the envisioned Late PPNB settlement of Ba'ja, another Neolithic site in the Petra-Mountains (see Kinzel 2013), and the sketched ground plans of the Minoan labyrinth, the Palladian Villa Rotonda, and Mies Van der Rohe's Barcelona Pavilion on page 40.

ON FOOD PRODUCTION AND MEALS – PLANTS, ANIMALS, AND THE ENVIRONMENT

Research on Neolithic and Palaeolithic food has a long tradition, but only with the recent introduction of use-wear analyses of ground stone tools and lithics to the study of Near Eastern archaeological material, we started to gain more valuable insights into past culinary customs. In the earlier days of archaeology, all finds were washed and cleaned before any study of the material took place. This meant that most traces of residues were removed before the analysis occurred, making it impossible to find traces of plant or animal remains. New analyses of phytoliths and proteins provide a more nuanced view of Neolithic nutrition (see P.56; Arranz Otaegui et al. 2018). The study of animal bone assemblages enables us to determine the number and species of animals that were consumed and, depending on the preservation of the bones, also the approximate age of the hunted game (Peters et al. 2012; Yeomans et al. 2017). Shkārat Msaied is a particularly interesting site when it comes to the transition from hunting and gathering to a herding- and farming-oriented lifestyle.

For her PhD, Pia Wistoft Nielsen is investigating the differences between herded animals that are still morphologically wild and those that are domesticated by looking at morphological changes over time in the animal bone assemblages found at Neolithic settlements. These changes developed over several generations before they manifested themselves in the archaeological data, and Shkārat Msaied falls within this transitional phase. Up to 80 % of the animal bones found at Shkārat Msaied are of goat, gazelle, and sheep. Goat dominates the faunal assemblage by far. Since the Petra area was a natural habitat for goats in the Pre-Pottery Neolithic, there are several challenges that make it difficult to establish whether the goats from Shkārat Msaied were wild and hunted or managed in some way (see P. 44 & 56). Both the ibex and the bezoar goat lived in the area; the bezoar is the wild progenitor of the domesticated goat whereas the ibex does not seem to have been herded. The only way to differentiate between the two species is by analysing the horn cores and not the bones.

Since the differentiation between the two species is still a challenge and complicates the analysis, we are left with little knowledge concerning the ratio of ibex and bezoar goats at the site. What we do know from the few horn cores that have been preserved, however, is that both ibex and bezoar goats were brought to and processed at Shkārat Msaied. One of the main questions for the study of the animal bones is whether goats might have been in the early stages of domestication at Shkārat Msaied. Unfortunately, given the fragile state of the bones and the sometimes impossible task of determining the species, this is still an unanswered question. What is obvious is that animals of various size and age were butchered at the site.

Mette Marie Hald's study of the botanical remains found at Shkārat Msaied suggests that the environment was more humid during the Neolithic than today. Especially the presence of some species of short-lived plants suggests this. The mountains were characterised by so-called open forests with stone oak, pistachio, and juniper trees. The denser tree cover may have been responsible for a low rate of erosion and higher degree of humidity. Some of the deep cut valleys and cliffs we see today were less steep and deep 10.000 years ago. In the graphic novel this denser tree cover is shown. The diversity of trees and plants is less visible in the story and not depicted in detail. This is intentional as research is still pending and we only have a very narrow window into the Neolithic flora so far. Studying archaeobotanical remains is one way that archaeologists investigate ancient food. The botanical material from Shkārat Msaied that has been analysed contained only a few species that could have been eaten, including emmer wheat and wild pistachio.

In addition, the presence of ground stone tools such as grinders and pounders suggests that these plants were processed further to serve as food (Harpelund 2011).

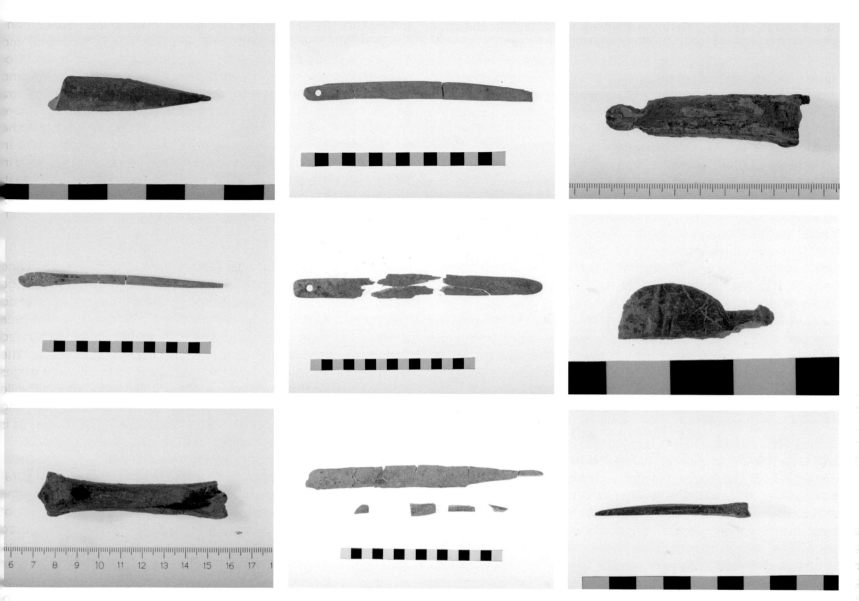

A selection of bone tools from Shkārat Msaied: awls, spatulae, figurines and needles
(photos: Pia Wistoft Nielsen/Shkārat Msaied Neolithic Project Archive)

In contrast to the relatively poor conservation of organic materials at Shkārat Msaied, objects made of non-organic materials, such as stone, are much better preserved. The raw material used to make flint tools came, according to Christoph Purschwitz (2017), not from the local sources in the immediate surroundings of the site. It was most probably collected from a site located at around 13 walking hours in distance from Shkārat Msaied, around the Neolithic flint mining field of, for example, Har Gevim (Gopher-Barkai 2011) on the western side of Wadi Araba. The tools were then produced at Shkārat Msaied by the individual households.

Gebel (1988) has written that nowadays there are no permanent springs within two walking hours of the site, although it is likely that there was a water source closer-by during the Neolithic. Still today, water can be found when one digs into the gravel beds of the wadi. It can be assumed that the water table was slightly higher during the Neolithic and that there was a spring close by. The area north of Shkārat Msaied has not been fully surveyed yet and may offer alternative explanations for where the inhabitants at the site collected their water. Natural cisterns have been found in the rock formations north of the settlement, which were heavily extended in Nabatean times (ca. 150 BCE to 105 CE).

BEADS AND TOOLS

With regard to other aspects of daily life in the Neolithic village of Shkārat Msaied, the excavations have revealed that some people at the site were engaged in the production of personal ornamentation such as beads. These beads were made from marine shells and a variety of stones. Most of the stone beads were made from greenstone, which appears to be either turquoise or malachite. Turquoise and malachite were also recovered as tiny fragments that probably represent the raw material or debitage from the production process. The nearest source for these greenstones would have been the Wadi Faynan/Wadi Fidan area, located about 25 km north of the settlement, or they might have come from the Sinai or the Negev desert. Roughouts of sandstone that represent unfinished beads were also recovered from the site. In the northern part of the excavation, two concentrations of flint drills have been found – as well as fragments of beads – together with debitage from the production of personal ornaments. Such drills were used in the production of flint tools and beads of different materials. These clusters attest to bead production within the settlement and have been interpreted as debris that might have been brushed off the roofs, which are assumed to have been the main activity areas within the settlement.

The most common type of bead was disc beads, but barrel beads, pendants, and one-cylinder beads were also found. This is probably because disc beads require fewer manufacturing steps and can be produced en masse. In Unit F, one large greenstone bead (Obj. 81311), possibly made of the mineral chrysoprase or chalcedony, was found in the fill of an almost empty burial cist (Loc. 80214), as depicted in the graphic novel. The burial cist contained only a few human and animal bone fragments. The greenstone bead surface was nicely polished and translucent. It measures 60.7 mm in length, 54.1 mm in width, and is 31.3 mm thick. The bead was longitudinally pierced with an 11.8 to 12.9 mm wide cylindrical shaft. The fact that it was found in the burial cist suggests that it was left there as part of a funerary rite.

Given the high density of finds related to bead production but low number of finished products found at the site, it has been suggested that the beads were utilised primarily outside the settlement as trade goods. Another reason why there is a lack of finished beads could be that people valued them highly and therefore took them along when they left the site; the blocked doorways (P.14 & 48) may attest to the settlement having been abandoned. Some scholars have suggested that the preference for greenstone, which is also apparent at other Pre-Pottery Neolithic sites in the Levant, indicates that this material probably had an embedded or symbolic meaning relating to vegetation and fertility (see Bar-Yosef Mayer & Porat 2008); however, this remains highly speculative. The bead manufacturing sequence presented on page 23 in the graphic novel is based on Roseleen Bains's (2012) work on the stone beads from the Neolithic site of Çatalhöyük (Turkey), and on experiments executed by Mette Bangsborg Thuesen (Thuesen & Kinzel 2018).

The vast majority of stone beads from Shkārat Msaied had evidence of bi-conical drilling, which means that the roughouts were drilled in a cone shape from both sides. Production marks from the polishing and the abrasion process were also visible, which are probably the result of ground stone tools being used to steady the beads during drilling and surface reduction.

More than one thousand ground stones were found during the excavation at Shkārat Msaied. Anne Mette Harpelund (2011) has divided these into twelve main categories depending on their shape and function. Ground stone tools constitute by far the largest assemblage at the site. The ground stone tools were probably used in different aspects of daily life, such as food preparation and processing, pigment processing, tool manufacturing and maintenance, plaster production as well as activities related to ceremonial events.

Beads and ground stone tools from Shkārat Msaied: (top) greenstone and sandstone beads; (left) two grinders – one with red pigments; (right) large greenstone bead (Obj. 81311) from an empty burial cist (Loc. 80214) (all photos: Shkārat Msaied Neolithic Project Archive).

TRANSFORMING THE DEAD

by Bo Dahl Hermansen

In the 2002 and 2003 seasons at Shkārat Msaied, the Danish expedition excavated a peculiar architectural feature inside a large circular building designated as Unit F (see P.67). Here, we unearthed the remains of a deceased individual that we determined to be a woman, some 35 years of age. The extremities of her body, i.e. legs and arms, had been severed from the rest of the body and deposited inside the rib cage, suggesting that the intestines had rotted away or simply been removed. The latter seems most likely when taking into consideration that the arms and legs were in full articulation. The skull and mandible had also been removed, but – contrary to the limbs – they were not found with the corpse. This led to the inevitable conclusion that the skull and mandible must have been deposited elsewhere – a common practice in the PPNB period (see time table, p. 53), to which the archaeological remains at Shkārat Msaied mostly belong. Interestingly, whereas the skull and mandible were absent, we found four sheep or goat mandibles deposited with the skeleton. In THE FOX, Moritz Kinzel and Konrad Nuka Godtfredsen tell one of many possible stories about this person.

Some of the deceased were given a special treatment after death. Their skulls were removed from the body and deposited separately. Depositing the skulls of selected deceased individuals was, in fact, one of the most spectacular practices of the PPNB period. Indeed, many excavated PPNB sites have revealed such skulls, severed from bodies and deposited – often collectively in caches. Interestingly, this practice was afforded persons of all sexes and ages. This tradition has frequently been called a 'skull cult' and is frequently believed to signify a prehistoric ancestor cult. However, specific case studies have suggested a broader range of possible practices to account for this peculiar phenomenon. We will discuss one of these in more detail below. At any rate, we submit that this phenomenon seems to be associated both with a shared practice, distributed throughout the wider region, and with features peculiar to each instance in which the practice has been documented archaeologically. Some skulls had been modified to become almost portrait-like: facial features had been suggested through plastering, painting, and through applying paint or even pastes to suggest hair or hairdos (P. 65). Eyes were sometimes indicated through the application of cowrie shells, nacre, or model coffee bean eyes. Ian Kuijt (2000) has shown that skulls are often found deposited in numbers of three or divisible by three, i.e. 3, 6…, but this is by no means universal.

This apparent focus on skulls is but the top of the iceberg when it comes to elaborate mortuary practices in the PPNB. In popular literature, little attention has been paid to the treatment of postcranial bones in PPNB mortuary practices, in spite of the fact that some interesting patterns in the evidence have suggested highly elaborate multistage practices in the transformation of the dead. Ian Kuijt (e.g. 2000) has shown beyond doubt that mortuary practices unfolded in elaborate, multistage, cyclical patterns. One such case is Shkārat Msaied, where the above-mentioned Unit F has revealed a treasury of evidence. In the following sections, I will describe the evidence in some detail and then offer an interpretation, which helped inspire Konrad Nuka and Moritz to create the visual universe and the storyline offered in THE FOX.

LIVING WITH THE DEAD

One of the buildings at Shkārat Msaied, Unit F, has been excavated extensively and revealed quite an impressive quantity of material relevant to our understanding of the relations between the living and the dead in the Neolithic community at Shkārat Msaied, exactly the relation around which our storyline revolves. Unit F (P.67) is roughly circular building with a floor area of roughly 25 m2. Its stone walls were found preserved to a height of up to 1.5 m. Its entryway opened towards the south and inside the door opening was found a remarkable feature, constructed of stones – briefly mentioned in the introductory remarks. This feature was set apart from the rest of the interior space by a 2 m long, vertical monolith and topped by a slab on which we found the remains of the woman described in the introduction (P.3, 14, 46). At the base of the vertical monolith, we found a small cache of three skulls, suggesting that the woman was not the only person at Shkārat Msaied who had her skull removed after death. Unfortunately, we do not know if any of these three skulls actually belonged to the woman. Beneath the floors of the building (several successive floors were identified, some plastered, others not), we unearthed a number of stone cists (P.31-32) with and without mortuary remains, mostly of adults, but subadults were also found.

Unit F itself was constructed in three main phases (p. 54), of which the earliest seems to be built directly on virgin soil. The latest version of the building is the largest and thereby incorporates the earlier phases in its own structure. Just outside Unit F, to the west of its entrance, was a small enclosure attached to it. Among the finds recovered from this small feature was a human figurine (P.55). We consider the stratigraphy of Unit F to suggest a deliberate attempt to conform with the past, possibly even with the village origins. The possible symbolic significance of this must be seen in close

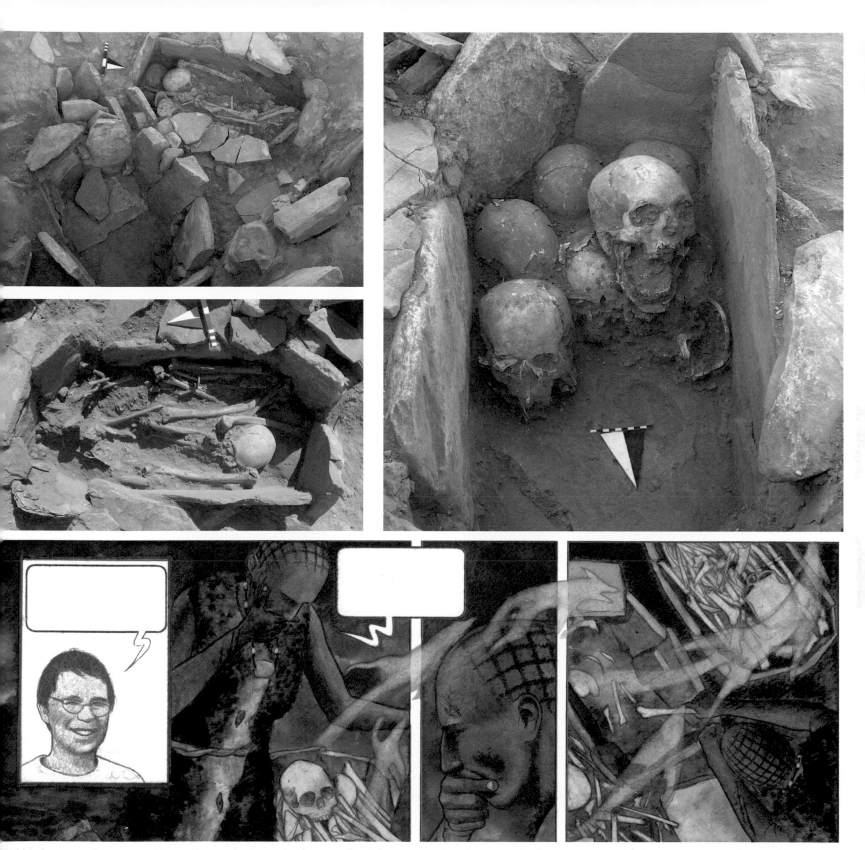

Multiple secondary burials in the eastern part of house Unit F. Body parts nicely sorted and separated (photos: Shkārat Msaied Neolithic Project Archive).

correlation with the funerary evidence recovered in Unit F and outlined below. In short, we interpret this house much in the same way as Ian Hodder's interpretation of the so-called 'history houses' at Çatalhöyük in Central Turkey (Hodder 2010). In the following, we shall review aspects of the mortuary evidence in more detail.

Sometime during the life cycle of Unit F, a number of subfloor cists were constructed. One of these (P.57) consisted of vertical stones set up as a frame for the skeletons of a minimum of eight dead individuals; six adults and two subadults. These bones had been carefully sorted. Seven skulls with mandibles were all laid down in a pile in the southern part of the pit, all looking towards the north (one of them – the last one to be deposited – with the mandible in articulation). One skull had been completely fragmented, and its remains were found scattered in the grave. Postcranial bones were deposited in the cist in a sorted fashion: a ribcage and vertebral column was laid down in the bottom of the grave in full anatomical articulation. The lower extremities of one individual were also deposited in anatomical order, but the left and right sides had been separated. Long bones were mostly laid down in a north-south direction in association with the flat bones, such as hips and scapulae, and then surrounded by vertebrae and ribs. It is important to note that there were no tool marks on the bones indicating that actually no active de-fleshing took place during mortuary practices.

Another cist with human bones had been reopened by the village inhabitants and its fill contained a disarticulated scatter of human bones. Interestingly, the fill on the floor in the vicinity of this cist contained a similarly disarticulated scatter of human bones. Two additional cists were found, both were open and except for a few scraps of human bones and a couple of beads, nothing was found in them. However, one of the beads (P.32, 71) was an extraordinarily large, green bead, which has been ascribed a special significance in THE FOX. Finally, a pit with infant skeletons was found as well.

From all this evidence we can say, first, that the corpses of the dead were manipulated in different states of disarticulation, suggesting that they represented individuals who died over a longer period. Some may have been relatively fresh, such as the body of the woman near the entryway of Unit F, whereas others had already experienced considerable decay, suggested by the fine sorting of bones in the first cist mentioned above. This again suggests that such funerary practices were a protracted process, recurring in cycles. This is one of the premises in THE FOX, which unfolds through part of the life of the main character, our 35-year-old female. In the tale, she initially buries the powerful old shaman of the village; then becomes initiated as a shaman herself, also a powerful one; and finally dies herself, to be subjected to a new sequence of funerary manipulation. This then heralds a future cycle in the story, which can only be conjectured from the archaeological findings since mortuary rites seem to have been discontinued, in the case of this corpse, simultaneously with the abandonment of the village itself.

The evidence outlined above clearly suggests that multistage mortuary practices were performed at Shkārat Msaied. Death, like birth, coming of age, marriage, etc., belongs to a special category of life events that we usually associate with social status transitions and are therefore generally considered to be critical. They are often associated with rites designed to smoothen the person's transition, so-called rites of passage or, in French, *rites-de-passage*. In a seminal volume from 1909, the Belgian historian of religion Arnold van Gennep demonstrated that such rites of passage often unfold in three stages (Van Gennep 1909). A *stage of separation* from the status group to which the person previously belonged; a *liminal stage* in which the person neither belonged to his/her previous status group nor to his/her future status group; and a *stage of incorporation* into the new status group. Each of these stages may be more or less pronounced and include more or less complex sequences of action in their own right. At Shkārat Msaied we may suggest that all three stages were elaborated, and that at least the second stage unfolded over several tempi.

If we stick to van Gennep's three-stage model here, we may suggest that at Shkārat Msaied the *first stage* – *separation* from society – may have taken place before bodies were cut into pieces. This may possibly have occurred outside Unit F in individual housing units or, given that some villagers must have died on their seasonal movements as the main character in THE FOX did, anywhere in the landscape. When the time had come, corpses would then be brought to Unit F where the dead were promoted collectively to the second stage in van Gennep's model – a *liminal stage* in between and betwixt life and death. In this stage, the dead travelled in the 'no man's land' between the living and the dead while belonging to neither category. They would have been considered a potential danger to society, perhaps the entire cosmic order, and the corpses would have been deemed to be polluted. Thus, the corpses were cut into pieces and rearranged as a collective entity in order to dissolve all individual existence and any risk of a return from the dead. They were then buried within a small chamber, such as Cist 1 (P.31, 57) described above. This cist was hermetically sealed by flat stone slabs providing an additional physical barrier to prevent return. The dead had now been transformed into a collective unit, which could – in due course – be promoted to the *third stage* in their *passage to the realm of the dead* (with the possible exception of those whose skulls were kept separate and manipulated in burial rites, whose names may have been retained during rites and remembered). In this stage

Dead body is found and brought back to the settlement. The body is prepared for the PASSAGE TO THE REALM OF THE DEAD.

RITES DE PASSAGE

DEATH/DECOMPOSING
Bodies are brought to a burial site in any state of decomposition.

STAGE 1 – SEPARATION:
Kin is parting with the dead. Bodies are likely to have been kept as intact as possible.

STAGE 2 – LIMINAL STAGE:
The dead are "in between and betwixt", hence a source of danger. Bones are sorted according to categories, dissolving individuality. Some skulls are kept separate. Placed in secure stone cists covered by stone slabs

STAGE 3 – INCORPORATION:
The dead have now been fully transformed. Human bones are completely mixed and even intermixed with animal bones. Bones of the dead could be removed or dispersed in floor fill.

The dead were now incorporated in their new status as a COLLECTIVE OF ANCESTORS. Thus, they were most probably considered as a source of life to society. A new cycle could then begin.

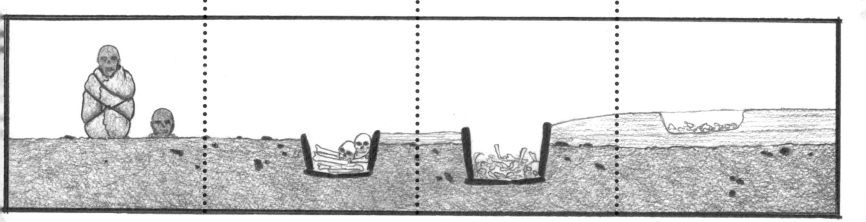

the bones were no longer considered to be dangerous. Cists, such as our Cist 2, could therefore be opened and the bones of the dead could be removed or dispersed in the floor fill as we see in Unit F. The dead were now properly incorporated into their new status as a collective of ancestors. Thus, they were most probably considered to be a source of life to society and could be approached ritually in case of any need. A new cycle could then begin.

Given the considerations above, the importance of such mortuary rites is beyond doubt, and we see this as highlighted in the finding of sheep/goat mandibles together with the female skeleton. This may suggest that mortuary rites were considered occasions for collective feasting with the dead as depicted in the graphic novel, a consideration that may perhaps be projected onto rites-de-passage in general.

RITUAL SPECIALISTS IN THE PPNB

As previously mentioned, the female body uncovered on top of the stone feature in Unit F was found without a skull and mandible. To remove the skull and mandible was a quite widespread practice in the PPNB, which was not afforded to all members of society. Which category of person that was given such a mortuary treatment in the PPNB is, of course, not known. However, it is an interesting fact that some severed skulls had been subjected to artificial deformation during infancy and childhood. This may suggest that these persons were recognised as special from very early on in their life, and that their status was 'stamped' on their bodies from early childhood through cranial deformation. Their status may have been inherited, but it may also have been ascribed to a child based on physical attributes, personality, or circumstances around their birth. We do not know the reason (however, see the discussion of vertical shamanism below). Nor do we know what extent of powers or authority was associated with this special status. What we do know is that the status, at least of individuals with deformed skulls, was 'stamped' onto their bodies throughout their lives. Many such deformed skulls were subjected to special treatment during mortuary rites. Thus, we may speculate that we are dealing with persons who had acted as mediators between planes of existence while alive and were expected to continue to do so during the transformation of themselves and their fellow deceased, i.e. these persons may have been ritual specialists, perhaps 'shamans'. This interpretation of the female body from the feature in Unit F lies at the heart of the characterisation and role of our main character in THE FOX. Due to the nature of this find, we do not know whether her head had been deformed or not, but other markers of status may also have been in use during the PPNB, such as mutilation, tattoos, hairdo, and body paint. Thus, in our story, we chose to give the woman a special haircut, which is based on

an applied net or haircut modelled on a PPNB skull from the site of Nahal Hemar (Bar Yosef & Alon 1988) in the Negev (P.65). This is of course speculative, but the association is certainly feasible.

The notion of 'shaman' originates with a category of ritual specialists in Siberia, who used altered states of consciousness to transcend between planes of existence, most often on behalf of members of their own societies. However, the Romanian historian of religion Mircea Eliade (1951) has shown that ritual specialists with similar powers practiced in regions throughout the world. Thus, 'shaman' has become the common name used to refer to that category of ritual specialist, which we will now characterise in short based on the work of Piers Vitebsky (1995), David Lewis-Williams and David Pearce (Lewis-Williams & Pearce 2005). Shamans are persons with special powers. They are selected by spirits, and after a sometimes long apprenticeship or learning phase they come to master one or more techniques of ecstasy, which enables the shaman to enter an artificially induced altered state of consciousness. In this condition the shaman´s soul will be able to travel between realms of existence. These are often conceptualised as a tiered cosmos by the shaman and his/her society. This cosmos often includes a netherworld where the dead exist alongside dangerous spirits. Then there may be a middle world, which is usually the home of humans, fauna, flora, etc. A third tier in the cosmos will often be an upper world where the main body of spirits lives and in some cases gods or, indeed, God. Shamanism is generally associated with notions that every entity in the cosmos is endowed with a spiritual force: a so-called animistic universe. Shamans are often thought to be able to change shape in their move between realms of existence, often into an animal. This may be an animal that possesses properties that allows it to mediate between worlds. E.g. the fox is an animal that hunts and lives much of its life in the middle world. However, it also lives much of its life in systems of subterranean caves, which brings foxes into close contact with the netherworld. This is the animal we have chosen as our shaman´s spirit animal for exactly the reasons outlined here and, of course, because a significant number of fox bones have been recovered from Unit F, the building in which our female skeleton was found.

Based on cross-cultural information, Lewis-Williams and Pearce (2005) have developed a model that proposes three increasingly deep states of altered consciousness. At least some of these are experienced by shamans entering a state of altered consciousness. In the first stage, the subject will often see geometrical patterns, such as sets of parallel lines, zigzag patterns, spirals, grid patterns, etc. In the second stage, he/she begins to make sense of these geometric patterns in terms of emotional or religious significance. Thus, referring to some of Lewis-Williams and Pearce´s examples, geometric shapes

SKELETRAPPORT Fundsted: Mus. nr.: AS 52/03

Grav nr. BM/SM 2003 50111 Scisa 52114

Udarbejdet af:_____

LÆNGDE FEMUR: h_____   v_____   Caput fem.: diam._____

LEGEMSHØJDE (udregnet):_____

KRANIUM: bredde: længde: Index: b x 100/l=

KØN: ?_____

Kranium:

Bækken:

Øvrige skelet:

ALDER: Adult_____

Kraniesuturer:

Tandslid:

Symphysis Pubica:

Ribben:

Øvrige skelet:

PATOLOGI:

Non observed !

Teeth:
• present
v lost post mortem
x e lost intra vitam
e erupting
0 not erupted

Excavation of the woman's skeleton in 2002 and 2003 (photos and locus sheet: Shkārat Msaied Neolithic Project Archive)

may become interwoven snakes, grids may become rigorously organised armies, and angular patterns may become houses or palaces with courts and gardens. Moving from the second to the third stage, the subject may have to pass through a vortex, e.g. in the form of a tunnel. Passing through this vortex to the third stage in the model, the subject enters a 'bizarre, ever-changing world of hallucinations' (Lewis-Williams and Pearce 2005: 54) experienced by all senses. This includes animals and the experience of changing from human to animal forms, exactly what we have tried to imply in the main character in THE FOX. Entering these states of altered consciousness is usually achieved through artificial means, such as singing, drumming, and dancing, but drugs and alcoholic beverages are often helpful as well. Interestingly, the imagery described in the model is characteristic of a wide range of animal, human, and geometric imagery from a large number of PPNB sites, including a few examples of geometric and human imagery from Shkārat Msaied (P.55). Three prominent properties of many shamans are their ability to heal, to provide plentiful hunting opportunities, and to be helpful in the transformation of the dead – including the ability to escort them on the way to their new destination in the netherworld. It is exactly these capacities that characterise the role played by our female shaman.

During his work in the Amazon Forest, British anthropologist Stephen Hugh-Jones (Hugh-Jones 1996; Lewis-Williams & Pearce 2005).) observed two kinds of shamanic systems. **HORIZONTAL SHAMANISM** and **VERTICAL SHAMANISM**. Horizontal Shamanism is relatively egalitarian. In such systems, shamans are mainly healers and providers of hunting game. The shaman´s individual experience is prominent, and his/her skills depend to a large extent on personal experience. In Horizontal Shamanism, rituals are often performed at the request of individuals. In Vertical Shamanism, on the other hand, a body of esoteric knowledge is passed down through generations within a small elite group. Here, apprenticeship is the main form of transmission of knowledge. Vertical Shamanism is typically associated with an esoteric system of religious beliefs and an increasingly hierarchical society in which shamans constitute a group of ritual specialists who perform regularly occurring rituals for the society at large. This would include rites of passage, such as those described here. It gives them a privileged position as a group and enables competition within the group. If it is possible to generalise from Hugh-Jones´ categories, it may be suggested that a form of shamanism akin to his Vertical Shamanism was beginning to emerge during the Middle PPNB, the period to which the occupation of Shkārat Msaied dates. And it is as a representative of the emerging system of Vertical Shamanism that we have envisaged our shaman in THE FOX as well as her predecessor and her successor, who both appear in the story.

MEMORY CULTURE AND SHAMANISM

Dismembering, sorting, and reassembling dead bodies; manipulating skulls; butchering goats and/or sheep and depositing them with corpses (feasting with the dead); and the deep architectural history of Unit F all suggests that the Neolithic inhabitants of this village considered death to be a transformation to another form of existence rather than simply the end of human life.

Indeed, this evidence is suggestive of what German memory scholar Jan Assmann (1992) has coined as 'memory culture'. According to Assmann, memory culture originated with the conscious experience of death as a radical and irreversible termination of life as we know it. Only with this conscious experience could the past come to acquire that otherness on which a memory culture can grow. Such a past 'must not have completely disappeared, there must be relics [… these relics must show a distinct difference to the "present"' (my translation from Assmann´s German (1992: 32)). To us, it seems clear that the evidence summarised above satisfy these conditions. As Assmann has also noted, claims are often made that the dead live on in memory. To him, however, the opposite is the case, i.e. the dead are deliberately revived through the collective will of the community in question. I have proposed elsewhere (Hermansen 2017) that such an act of revival is exactly what the evidence from Shkārat Msaied suggests: an act of reviving the dead by promoting them to a new state of being. Here 'ritual specialists' such as the main character in THE FOX might then approach them. In that respect, it is probably more than a coincidence that a widespread claim made by shamans worldwide is that their initiation involves the subjective experience of being dismembered and then reassembled into human shape, now transformed to their new status of a shaman.

This frequently occurring shamanic experience may well be related to the practice, also observed at Shkārat Msaied, of dismembering the dead and then reassembling them, in this case as a collective body of dead ancestors. Dismembering and reassembling skeletons, then, are the symbols of death and revival as constituent members of their new status group. This allows us to return to our ritual specialist in THE FOX. One role frequently seen among shamans (see above), is that they are believed to be able to escort the dead to their new destination. This is the role that we cautiously – in the graphic novel perhaps less cautiously – ascribe to at least some of those whose skulls received special treatment in the mortuary rites at PPNB sites. Possibly someone like our woman in THE FOX.

Reconstruction of the Pre-Pottery Neolithic B settlement at Shkārat Msaied/Jordan (M.Kinzel 2013).

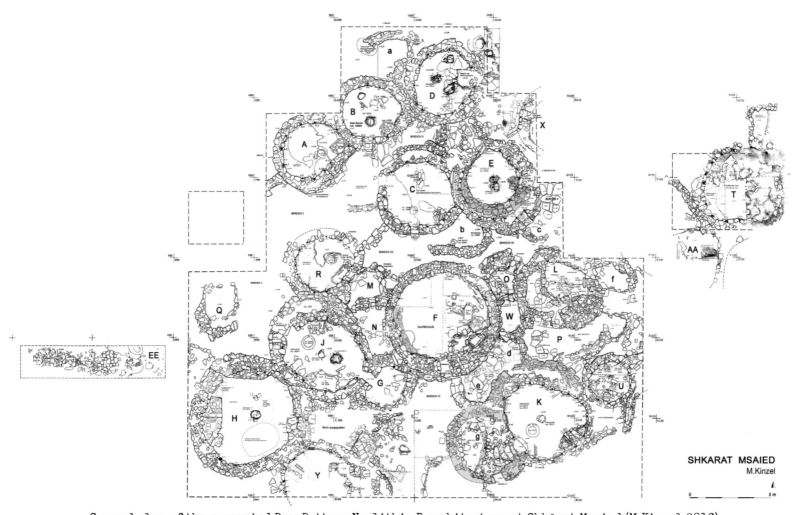

SHKARAT MSAIED
M.Kinzel

0   5 m

Ground plan of the excavated Pre-Pottery Neolithic B architecture at Shkārat Msaied (M.Kinzel 2016).

REFERENCES

ON SHKARAT MSAIED

Hermansen, B.D. et al. 2006. Shkarat Msaied: The 2005 season of excavations. A short preliminary report. Neo-Lithics 1/06: 3-7

Jensen, C.H. 2002. Verdens ældste landsby? Sfinx 25,4: 168-171.

Jensen, C.H. et al.2005. Preliminary report on the excavations at Shkarat Al-Musayid, 1999-2004. Annual of the Department of Antiquities of Jordan. Vol. 49: 115-134

Kaliszan, L.R et al. 2002. Shaqarat Mazyad - The village on the edge. Neo-Lithics 2/02: 16-19

Kinzel, M. 2018 Neolithic Shkārat Msaied - latest results. In: Z. M. Al-Salameen and M. B. Tarawneh (eds.): Refereed Proceedings of the First Conference on the Archaeology and Tourism of the Maan Governorate, 3rd- 4th October, 2017. Petra- Jordan; Supplement to Al-Hussein Bin Talal University's Journal of Research, AHUJ Deanship of Scientific Research and Graduate Studies, Al-Hussein Bin Talal University. 2018: 93-104.

Kinzel, M. 2018. Petra: Shkārat Msaied. In: Green, J.D.M., Porter, B.A., and Shelton C.P. (eds.) 2018. Archaeology in Jordan Newsletter: 2016 and 2017 Seasons.ACOR: Amman, Jordan. p. 69-70.

Kinzel, M. 2016. Petra: Shkārat Msaied. In: G.J. Corbett, D.R. Keller, B.A.Porter, and C.P. Shelton: Archaeology in Jordan. 2014 and 2015 seasons. In: American Journal of Archaeology vol. 120 no. 4, 2016. DOI: 10.3764/aja.120.4.0631. Archeological Institute of America: 2016: 659-660. http://www.ajaonline.org/newsletter/3182

Kinzel, M. 2008. Preservation and presentation of Neolithic sites: A case study at Shkarat Msaied, Southern Jordan. In Marchetti, N & Thuesen I. (eds.) ARCHAIA Case studies on research planning, characterisation, conservation and management of archaeological sites. Bar Int. Ser. 1877: 331-340

Kinzel M. - Abu Laban A. - Hoffmann Jensen C. - Thusesn I. - Jørkov M. 2011 Insights into PPNB architectural transformation, human burials, and initial conservation works: Summary on the 2010 excavation season at Shkārat Msaied. Neo-Lithics 1/11: 44-49.

Kinzel M., Harpelund A.M., Jørkov M.L.S., Nielsen P.W., Purschwitz C., Soria A.H., Thuesen M.B., and Thuesen I. 2020. Life and Death at Shkārat Msaied: Results of the 2014 and 2015 seasons. In: Studies in History and Archaeology of Jordan (ICHAJ 2016), Proceedings of the 13th International Conference on the History and Archaeology of Jordan (21st – 26th May, 2016), Amman. 503-512.

Kinzel M. - Hwawra K. - Nielsen P. - Harpelund A.M. - Hellum J. - Thuesen M. - Thuesen I., 2015. Shkārat Msaied 2014: Summary of results. http://www.damaskus.dk/shkarat-msaied-2014-summary-of-results/ [15-05-2015].

Kinzel M. - Bakkar L. - Godtfredsen K.N. - Harpelund A.M. - Hellum J.K. - Hwawra K. - Jørkov M.L.S. - Nielsen P.W. - Purschwitz C. -Thuesen I. - Thuesen M.B. -Soria A.H. 2016. Shkārat Msaied, the 2014 and 2015 Seasons. In: Neo-Lithics 2/15: 3-10.

Kinzel M. - Jørkov M.L. - Stråhlén R. - Thuesen M.B. - Thuesen I. 2017 Shkārat Msaied 2016: New results from Unit F. In: Neo-Lithics 01/2017: 13-17

ON THE NEAR EASTERN NEOLITHIC

Benz, M. - Gebel, H.G.K. - Watkins, T. (eds.) 2017. Neolithic Corporate Identitie SENESPSE 20. Berlin: ex oriente.

Garfinkel, Y. 2003. Dancing at the Dawn of Agriculture. Austin: University of Texsa Press

Gebel, H.G. 1986. Die Jungsteinzeit im Petra-Gebiet. In: M. Lindner (ed.): Petra - Neu Ausgrabungen und Entdeckungen. München: Delp. 273-308.

Gebel, H.G.K. 1988. Late Epipalaeolithic - Aceramic Neolithic sites in the Petra are In: Garrard, A. N., and H. G. Gebel 1988 The prehistory of Jordan: the state of researc in 1986. BAR International Series 396. Oxford: British Archaeological Press. 67-100.

Hauptmann, H. 2011. The Urfa Region. In: M. Özdoğan - N. Başgelen - P. Kuniholr (eds.): The Neolithic in Turkey 2 – The Euphrates Basin. Istanbul: Archaeology and A Publications. 85-138.

Hermansen, B.D. 2014. Byen før byen. Landsbyliv I tidlig neolitikum. By og kultur, 74-80.

Hermansen, B.D. 2009. Capturing vertical space. In: H.G.K.Gebel - Z.Kafafi - O.Ghu (eds.): Modesty and Patience. Studies in Honour of Nabil Qadi "Abu Salim Monographs of the Faculty of Archaeology and Anthropology Vol.20. Irbid: Yarmou University, and Berlin: ex oriente, S.42-48.

Hermansen, B.D. 2003. Towards New Frameworks: Supra-Regional Concepts in Nea Eastern Neolithization. Introductory remarks. Neo-Lithics 2/2003: 32-33. Ex Oriente Berlin.

Hermansen, B.D. 2004. Supra-Regional Concepts from a Local Perspective. Neo Lithics 1/2004:34-38. Ex Oriente, Berlin.

Kirkbride, D. 1966. Five seasons at the prepottery Neolithic village of Beidha, Jordan Palestine Exploration Quarterly 98: 5-61.

Özbaşaran, M. - Duru, G. - Stiner, M. (eds.) 2018. The early settlement at Aşıklı Höyük Essays in Honor of Ufuk Esin. Istanbul: Ege Yayinlari.

Schrenk, F. 2009. Vom aufrechten Gang zur Kunst - Die Entwicklung und Ausbreitung des Menschen. In: Archäologisches Landmuseum Baden-Württemberg (ed.): Eiszeí - Kunst und Kultur. Begleitband zur Großen Landesausstellung Eiszeit - Kunst und Kultur im Kunstgebäude Stuttgart 18.September 2009 bis 10. Januar 2010. Stuttgart Thorbecke. 52 -60.

Simmons, A. 2007. The Neolithic Revolution in the Near East. Transforming the Human Landscape. Tucson: University of Arizona Press.

Stordeur, D. 2015. Le village de jerf el Ahmar (Syrie, 9500 - 8700 av. J.-c.). L'architecture miroir d'une société néolithique complexe. Paris: CBRS.

Thuesen I. 2008. Og Gud skabte mennesket i sit billede... In: Ny Carlsberg Glyptotek (ed.): Tidernes morgen: på sporet af kulturens kilder i det gamle Mellemøsten Copenhagen: Meddelelser fra Ny Carlsberg Glyptotek nr. 10:9-17.

N ARCHITECTURE

anning, E.B. - Chazan, M. (eds.) 2006. Domesticating Space: Construction, ommunity, and Cosmology in the Late Prehistoric Near East, SENEPSE 12. Berlin: x oriente.

lle Petersen, M. 2003. Social Interaction in a Prehistoric Settlement. A study f Social Interaction from an architectural perspective in the MPPNB society of haqarat Masiad in Southern Jordan. MS thesis, University of Copenhagen

yrd, B. F. 2005. Early Village Life at Beidha, Jordan: Neolithic Spatial Organization nd vernacular Architecture. The excavations of Mrs. Diana Kirkbride-Helbæk. eidha Excavations No. 2. British Academy Monographs in Archaeology No. 14. xford: CBRL/Oxford University Press.

ebel, H.G. 2006. The Domestication of Vertical Space: The Case of Steep-Slope PPNB Architecture in Southern Jordan. In: E B. Banning and Michael Chazan (eds.): omesticating Space - Construction, Community, and Cosmology in the Late rehistoric Near East. SENEPSE 6. Berlin: ex oriente.

ebel H.G.K. - Nissen H.J. - Zaid, Z. 2006. Basta II - The Architecture and Stratigraphy. ibliotheca Asiae meridionalis et occidentalis Vol. 5, Berlin: ex oriente.

inzel, M. 2019. 'Special buildings' at Shkārat Msaied. In: Nakamura, S., Adachi, T., and be M. (eds), Decades in Deserts: Essays on Western Asian Archaeology in Honor of umio Fujii: 79–94. Tokio: Rokuichi Shobo.

inzel, M. 2014. Überlegungen zur Raumgestaltung und Wegeführung in der eolithischen Architektur Südjordaniens. In: Kurapkat, D., Wulf-Rheidt, U. (eds.): ie Architektur des Weges - Gestaltet Bewegung im gebauten Raum: Diskussionen ur Archäologischen Bauforschung Internationales Kolloquium in Berlin vom 7. is 11. Februar 2012 veranstaltet vom Architekturreferat des DAI Diskussionen zur rchäologischen Bauforschung 11, Berlin 2013. Regensburg: Schnell und Steiner 014: 269-288.

inzel, M. 2013. Am Beginn des Hausbaus. Studien zur PPNB-Architektur von Shkārat saied und Ba'ja in der Petra-Region, Jordanien. SENEPSE 17, Berlin: ex oriente.

inzel, M. 2008 Take a look, make a sketch and re-think it: Surveying and 4D models or reconstructing archaeological sites. In Marchetti, N & Thuesen I. (eds.) ARCHAIA ase studies on research planning, characterisation, conservation and management f archaeological sites. Bar Int. Ser. 1877: 91-100

inzel, M. 2007. Early Neolithic Building in the Southern Levant: The PPNB rchitecture of Shkarat Msaied and Ba'ja, Neo-Lithics 1/07:51.

inzel, M. 2005. Jungsteinzeitliches Bauen in Südjordanien. Architekten- und ngenieurverein zu Berlin 1: 55-59.

inzel, M. 2004. Some notes on the reconstruction of PPNB architecture. Neo-Lithics /04: 18-22.

inzel, M. – Duru, G. – Barański, M. Z., 2020. Modify to last – a Neolithic perspective n rebuilding and continuation. In Piesker, K. - Wulf-Reidt, U. (eds.) Umgebaut: iskAB13. Regensburg, Schnell & Steiner.

Kurapkat, D. 2015. Frühneolithische Sondergebäude auf dem Göbekli Tepe in Obermesopotamien und vergleichbare Bauten in Vorderasien. PhD. Technical University Berlin.

Kurapkat, D. 2014. Bauwissen im Neolithikum Vorderasiens. In, Renn, J., Osthues, W. and Schlimme, H (eds), Wissensgeschichte der Architektur: Band I: Vom Neolithikum bis zum Alten Orient. [e-book] Berlin: Edition Open Access/Max Planck Institute for the History of Science. Available at: <http://edition-open-access.de/media/studies/3/4/stud3ch4.pdf> [Accessed April 17 2018].

Mithen, S., Finlayson, B., Maricevic, D., Smith, S., Jenkins, E. and Najjar, M. (eds.) 2019. WF16: Excavations at an Early Neolithic Site in Southern Jordan, London: Council for British Research in the Levant 2019.

ON FEASTING, MEMORY, MAGIC RITUALS, SHAMANISM, AND MORTUARY PRACTICES

Assmann J. 1992. Das kulturelle Gedächtnis: Schrift, Erinnerung und politische Identität in frühen Hochkulturen. Munich: Verlag C.H. Beck.

Bar Yosef O. & Alon D. 1988. Nahal Hemar: The Excavations´. Atiqot 18.

Bar-Yosef, O. 1985. A cave in the Desert - Nahal Hemar. Jerusalem: The Isreal Museum.

Benz, M. 2006. Zur Bedeutung von Festen während der Neolithisierung im Voderen Orient. In: EAZ, Ethnogr.-Archäol. Z. 47, 2006, p. 439-462.

Eliade M. 1951/1964. Shamanism: Archaic Techniques of Ecstacy. (English Translation by W. R. Trask) Princeton: Princeton University Press.

Gebel H.G.K. - Hermansen, B.D. - Jensen, C.H. (eds.) 2002 (2004). Magic Practices in the Early Near Eastern Neolithic. Production, Subsistence, and Environment and Ritual on the Near Eastern Neolithic. 8. Ex Oriente, Berlin

Gennep A. van 1909/1969. Les rites de passage. Rééditions maison de sciences de l´homme, 5. New York: Johnson Reprint corporation; Paris, la Haye: Mouton.

Hermansen B.D. 2017. Death, Feasting, and Memory Culture at Early Neolithic Shkarat Msaied, Southern Jordan´. In: L. Bredholt Christensen & J. Tae Jensen (eds.), Religion and Material Culture: Studying Religion and Religious Elements on the Basis of Objects, Architecture, and Space. pp.169-197. Turnhout, Belgium: Brepols.

Hermansen, B.D. 2008. Liv og død i en stenalderlandsby. In: Ny Carlsberg Glypotek (ed.): Tidernes morgen: på sporet af kulturens kilder i det gamle Mellemøsten. Copenhagen: Meddelelser fra Ny Carlsberg Glyptotek nr. 10:18-24.

Hermansen, B.D. - Jensen, C.H. 2002 (2004). Notes on some features of possible ritual significance at MPPNB Shqarat Mazyad, Southern Jordan. In: Gebel, H.G. - Hermansen, B.D. - Jensen, C.H. (eds.) Magic practices and ritual in the Near Eastern Neolithic. Studies in Early Near Eastern Production, Subsistence, and Environment 8: 91-101. Ex. Oriente, Berlin.

Hodder, I. & Pels, P. 2010. 'History houses: a new interpretation of architectural elaboration at Çatalhöyük'in I. Hodder (ed.), Religion in the emergence of civilization. Çatalhöyük as a case study. Cambridge: Cambridge University Press.

Hugh-Jones S. 1996. ´Shamans, Prophets, Priests, and Pastors. In: N. Thomas & C. Humphrey (eds.), Shamanism: History and the State. Ann Arbor: University of Michigan Press.

Kenyon, K. 1953. Neolithic Portait-Skulls from Jericho. in: Antiquity, 106: 105-107.

Kuijt I. 2000. Keeping the Peace: Ritual, Skull Caching, and Community Integration in the Levantind Neolithic´. In: I. Kuijt (ed.) Life in Neolithic Farming Communities: Social Organization, Identity, and Differentiation. New York: Kluwer Academic/ Plenum Publishers.

Lewis-Williams D. & Pearce D. 2005. Inside the Neolithic Mind: Consciousness, Cosmos, and the Realm of the Gods. London: Thames & Hudson.

Vitebski P. 1995. The Shaman: Voyages of the Soul, Ecstasy and Healing from Siberia to the Amazon. London: MacMillan.

Schmandt-Besserat D. 2013. The Plastered Skulls. In: D. Schmandt-Besserat (ed.): Symbols at 'Ain Ghazal. 'Ain Ghazal Excavation Reports Vol. 3. Berlin: ex oriente. 213-243.

ON SMALL FINDS, JEWLLERY, GROUND STONES, AND CHIPPED STONE

Abu-Laban, A. 2010. Analysis and reconstruction of the use of mollusc shells from the MPPNB site Shkarat Msaied in Southern Jordan. MS thesis, University of Copenhagen.

Abu-Laban. A. 2014. The use of marine mollusc shells at the Neolithic site Shkarat Msaied, Jordan. In (eds.) Proceedings of the Archaeomalacology Session, 11th ICAZ Conference. BAR Int. Series. 2666: 9-17.

Andresen M. 2007 Abiotische Rohstoffe in der frühneolithischen Siedlung Ba'ja (Jordanien). Unpublished Magisterarbeit. Universität Heidelberg.

Bains, R. 2012. The Social Significance of Neolithic Stone Bead Technologies at Çatalhöyük. London: UCL. Accessible at: http://discovery.ucl.ac.uk/1368215/ [assessed: 27.05.2019].

Gopher A. - Barkai R. 2011. A New Neolithic Quarry Complex at Har Gevim, Israel: An Introduction. In: Proceedings Of The 2nd Conference Of The Uispp Commission On Flint Mining.

Harpelund, A.M., 2011. An analysis of the ground stone assemblage from the Middle Pre-Pottery Neolithic B site Shkarat Msaied in Southern Jordan. MA-thesis, University of Copenhagen.

Jensen, C.H. 2008. Workshops and activity areas in the PPNB period: The excavations at Shkarat Msaied. In: Kühne, H. et al. (eds.) Proceedings of the Fourth International Congress on the Archaeology of the Ancient Near East (2004). Vol. 2. 2008 Berlin: Harrassowitz Verlag. p. 331-344.

Jensen, C.H. 2004. Productions areas at MPPNB Shkarat Msaied, Southern Jordan. Neo-Lithics 2/04: 22-26

Purschwitz C. 2013. Ba'ja 2012: Abiotic Resources and Early Neolithic Raw Materi[...] Procurement in the Greater Petra Area (ARGPA) - Research Aims and First Result[...] Neo-Lithics 1/13: 3-10.

Purschwitz C. 2016a. Shkârat Msaied. A MPPNB bidirectional blade workshop and i[...] socioeconomic implications. Poster presented at the 8th International Conferenc[...] on Pre Pottery Neolithic Chipped and Ground Stone Industries of the Near Eas[...] November 23rd – 27th 2016 Nicosia, Cyprus.

Purschwitz C. 2016b. The Lithological Landscape of the Greater Petra Regio[...] Availability of Flint and other Abiotic Ressources. Poster presented at 8[...] International Conference on Pre Pottery Neolithic Chipped and Ground Stor[...] Industries of the Near East. November 23rd – 27th 2016 Nicosia, Cyprus.

Purschwitz, C. 2017. Die lithische Ökonomie von Feuerstein im Frühneolithiku[...] der Größeren Petra Region, Südlevante. Studies in Early Near Eastern Productio[...] Subsistence, and Environment 19. Berlin: ex oriente.

Quintero, L. 2010. Evolution of Lithic Economies in the Levantine Neolithi[...] Development and Demise of Naviform Core Technology as Seen from 'Ain Ghaz[...] 'Ain Ghazal Excavation Reports Vol. 2. Berlin: ex oriente.

Quintero, L.A. - Wilke, P. J.- Waines, J.G. 1997. Pragmatic Studies of Near Easter[...] Neolithic Sickle Blades. In: H.G.K. Gebel - Z. Kafafi - G.O. Rollefson (eds.): The Prehistor[...] of Jordan, II. Perspectives from 1997. SENEPSE 4. Berlin: exoriente. p.263-286.

Stordeur, D. 1988. L'industrie osseuse de Çafer dans son contexte anatolien [...] proche oriental. Note préliminaire. Anatolica , XV, pp. 203-213.

Thuesen, M. E. B. - Kinzel, M. 2018. Stone Beads from Shkarat Msaied. Neo-Lithic[...] 1/18: e3-e7.

Wilke, P.J. - Quintero, L. - Gebel, H.G.K. 2014. Flint 'Bowl-lets' and the issue of Artificia[...] Lighting in neolithic Jordan. In: B. Finlayson - C. Makarewicz (eds.): Settlemen[...] Survey, and Stone. Essays on Near Eastern Prehistory in Honour of Gary Rollefso[...] Berlin: ex oriente 2014: 219-226.

ON BOTANICAL AND FAUNAL REMAINS

Arranz-Otaeguia, A. -Gonzalez Carreterob L. - Ramsey M.N.- Fuller, D. Q. - Richter,[...] 2018. Archaeobotanical evidence reveals the origins of bread 14,400 years ago i[...] northeastern Jordan. PNAS, vol. 115, no. 31, 7925–7930.

Bangsgaard, P. 2008. An introduction to faunal remains and environmental studie[...] A mismatch or match made in heaven? In Marchetti, N & Thuesen I. (eds.) ARCHAI[...] Case studies on research planning, characterisation, conservation and managemer[...] of archaeological sites. Bar Int. Ser. 1877: 231-237

Bangsgaard, P. 2005. Rituel brug af oldgamle fugle i Jordan. Dyr i natur og museun[...] 2005/ 1: 6-10. København: Zoologisk Museum.

Bangsgaard Jensen, P. 2005. An Analysis of the Faunal Material from the MPPNB sit[...] of Shaqarat Masiad in Southern Jordan. MS thesis, University of Copenhagen.

...ar, V. 2003. An Analysis of the Relations between Arrowhead Groups and larger ...ild Animal Species at Shaqarat Masiad and other PPNB sites of the Southern ...evant. MS thesis, University of Copenhagen.

...ielsen, P., 2014. Just another bone tool or an open window to the social organisation ...f production in the PPNB? An analysis of the bone industry from Shkarat Msaied ...MPPNB). MS thesis/speciale, University of Copenhagen.

...ielsen, P., 2009. Worked bones in the Pre-Pottery Neolihtic B (PPNB) from the ...outhern Levant. An analysis and comparison of the bone industries of the two sites ...liddle PPNB Shakarat Masiad and Late PPNB site Ba'ja. MA thesis. The University of ...dinburgh.

...eters, J. – Arbuckle, B.S. – Pöllath, N. 2012. Subsistence and beyond: Animals in ...eolithic Anatolia. In: M. Özdogan - N. Basgelen - P. Kuniholm (eds.) THE NEOLITHIC ...I TURKEY, VOL. 6, Archaeology and Art Publications, Istanbul 2012, pp. 1-65.

...eters, J. - Schmidt K. 2004. Animals in the symbolic world of Pre-...otteryNeolithic Göbekli Tepe, south-eastern Turkey: a preliminary assessment. ...NTHROPOZOOLOGICA 2004. 39 (1).Paris: Muséum national d'Histoire naturelle, p. ...79 - 218.

...eomans, L. M. - Martin, L. -Richter, T. 2017. Environment, seasonality and hunting ...trategies as influenceson Natufian food procurement: The faunal remains from ...hubayqa 1. Levant: The Journal of the Council forBritish Research in the Levant, ...9(2), 85-104.

...N CLOTHING

...eckinger, A. 2007. Ötzi, der Mann aus dem Eis. Wien/Bozen: Folio Verlag.

...römer, K. 2010. Prähistorische Textilkunst in Mitteleuropa – Geschichte ...es Handwerks und der Kleidung vor den Römern. Veröffentlichungen der ...rähistorischen Abteilung des Naturhistorischen Museums 4. Wien: Verlag des ...aturhistorischen Museums.

...evy, J. 2020. The Genesis of the Textile Industry from Adorned Nudity to Ritual ...egalia. Oxford: Archaeopress.

...iennicka, M. - Rahmsdorf, L. - Ulanowska, A. (eds.) 2018. First Textiles: The Beginnings ...f Textile Manufacture in Europe and the Mediterranean. Oxford: Oxbow.

...Valter 2009. Eiszeitliche Kleidung rekonstruiert. In: Archäologisches Landmuseum ...aden-Württemberg (ed.): Eiszeit - Kunst und Kultur. Begleitband zur Großen ...andesausstellung Eiszeit - Kunst und Kultur im Kunstgebäude Stuttgart ...8.September 2009 bis 10. Januar 2010. Stuttgart: Thorbecke. 176 - 179.

...ulzenbacher G. 2008. Die Gletschermumie. Mit Ötzi auf Entdeckungsreise durch ...ie Jungsteinzeit. Wien / Bozen: Folio Verlag.

ARCHAEOLOGY, NARRATIVES, AND GRAPHICS

Godtfredsen, K. N. with Grønnow, B. and Sørensen, M. , 2009. The First Steps. Nuuk: Ilinniusiorfik.

Godtfredsen, K.N. and Appelt, M. 2012, The Ermine. Nuuk: Ilinniusiorfik.

Godtfredsen, K. N. and Valgreen, L. with Gulløv, H.C. 2015, The Gift. Nuuk: Ilinniusiorfik.

Godtfredsen, K. N., and Valgreen, L. with Arneborg, J., 2018. The Scar. Nuuk: Ilinniusiorfik.

Helle, M.P. 2009. Hej menneske. Copenhagen: Lindhardt og Ringhof.

Macaulay, D. 1979. Motel of the Mysteries. New York: Houghton Mifflin.

Swogger J. 2015. Ceramics, Polity and Comics - Visually representing formal archaeological publication. Advances in Archaeological Practice, Vol. 3 No. 1, 2015.

WEBLINKS TO RESEARCH PROJECTS

Shkarat Msaied Neolihtic Project: https://shkaratmsaied.tors.ku.dk/

Ba'Ja Neolithic Project: https://www.exoriente.org/baja/

Shubayqa - Project: https://shubeika.ccrs.ku.dk/

Asikli Höyük Project: http://www.asiklihoyuk.org/

Catalhöyük Project: http://www.catalhoyuk.com/

Göbekli Tepe Project: https://www.dainst.org/projekt/-/project-display/21890

Centre for the Study of Early Agricultural Societies: https://cseas.ku.dk/

Konrad Nuka Godtfredsen: https://www.andalaworld.com/

Acknowledgments:

We have to thank several people and institutions for supporting this project:

the Department of Antiquities of Jordan for their long-standing support
the Amareen of Beidha for their friendship and fine excavation work
the Nawafleh Family at Wadi Musa for their hospitality
ex oriente e.V. Berlin and the Ba'ja Neolihic Project
Tobias Richter, Lisa Yeomans, and Amaia Arranz Otaegui of the Shubayqa Project
the Centre for the Study of Early Agricultural Societies – CSEAS, University of Copenhagen
the Ashby family, Empshott, UK
the Göbekli Tepe Project, German Archaeological Institute – Şanliurfa Müzesi

For financial support we are grateful to
the Danish Ministry of Education and Research
the Danish Institute in Damascus
the Danish Palestine Foundation (H.P. Hjerl-Hansen Mindefondet for Dansk Palæstinaforskning)
the Department of Cross-Cultural and Regional Studies, University of Copenhagen

Uddannelses- og
Forskningsministeriet

المعهد الدنماركي بدمشق

DET DANSKE INSTITUT I DAMASKUS

KØBENHAVNS
UNIVERSITET